Transforming Preaching

TRANSFORMATIONS
THE EPISCOPAL CHURCH IN THE 21ST CENTURY

Transforming Preaching

RUTHANNA B. HOOKE

Church Publishing
NEW YORK

Library of Congress Cataloging-in-Publication Data
Hooke, Ruthanna.
Transforming preaching / Ruthanna Hooke.
    p. cm.
Includes bibliographical references (p.).
ISBN 978-0-89869-646-2 (pbk.)
1. Episcopal preaching (Episcopal Church) I. Title.
BX5979.5.P73H66 2010
251'.01—dc22
                                        2010001384

Cover design by Stefan Killen Design
Study guide and interior design by Vicki K. Black

Printed in the United States of America

Church Publishing, Incorporated
445 Fifth Avenue
New York, New York 10016
www.churchpublishing.org

5   4   3   2   1

Contents

a note from the publisher

This series emerged as a partnership between
the Office of Mission of the Episcopal
Church and Church Publishing, as a contribution to the mission of the church in a new
century. We would like to thank James
Lemler, series editor, for bringing the initial
idea to us and for facilitating the series. We
also want to express our gratitude to the
Office of Mission for two partnership
grants: the first brought all the series authors
together for two creative days of brain-
storming and fellowship; and the second is
helping to further publicize the books of the
series to the clergy and lay people of the
Episcopal Church.

Series Preface

B e ye transformed" (KJV). "Be transformed by the renewing of your minds" (NRSV). "Fix your attention on God. You'll be changed from the inside out" (*The Message*). Thus St. Paul exhorted the earliest Christian community in his writing to the Romans two millennia ago. This exhortation was important for the early church and it is urgent for the Episcopal Church to heed as it enters the twenty-first century. Be transformed. Be changed from the inside out.

Perhaps no term fits the work and circumstances of the church in the twenty-first century better than "transformation." We are increasingly aware of the need for change as we become ever more mission-focused in the life of the church, both internationally and domestically. But society as a whole is rapidly moving in new directions, and mission cannot be embraced in an unexamined way, relying on old cultural and ecclesiastical stereotypes and assumptions.

This new series, *Transformations: The Episcopal Church in the 21st Century*, addresses these issues in realistic and hopeful ways. Each book focuses on one area within the Episcopal Church that is urgently in need of transformation in order for the church to be effective in the twenty-first century: vocation, evangelism, preaching, congregational life, getting to know the Bible, leadership, Christian formation, worship, and stewardship. Each volume explains why a changed vision is essential, gives robust theological and biblical foundations, offers guidelines to best practices and positive trends, describes the necessary tools for change, and imagines how transformation will look.

Transformed and authoritative preaching is vital for the present and future life of the church. For Ruthanna Hooke, preaching is the opportunity for our story to be further grounded in God's story: God is not only active in preaching, but present in a particularly powerful and sacramental way. *Transforming Preaching* explores why preaching is so difficult, and provides essential models and spiritual practices to transform both the creators and hearers of sermons. Hooke discusses the use of body, breath, and voice in preaching, and includes insightful interviews with some of the most accomplished preachers in the church today, who talk about their vocation and the distinctive challenges that this calling presents to them.

Like Christians in the early church, today we live in a secular culture that can be apathetic and even hostile to Christianity. Living in a setting where people are not familiar with the message or narrative of Christian believing requires new responses and new kinds of mission for the body of Christ. We believe this is a hopeful time for spiritual seekers and inquirers in the church. The gospel itself is fresh for this century. God's love is vibrant and real; God's mission can transform people's hopes and lives. Will we participate in the transformation? Will we be bearers and agents of transformation for others? Will we ourselves be transformed? This is the call and these are the urgent questions for the Episcopal Church in the twenty-first century.

But first, seek to be transformed. Fix your attention on God. You'll be changed from the inside out.

JAMES B. LEMLER, *series editor*

Acknowledgments

It is a joy to thank the many people who have been involved in contributing to this book and encouraging it into print. Thanks are due in the first instance to Peter Hawkins, who proposed my name as a contributor to this *Transformations* series. A meeting at the outset of this process with the other writers in this series was helpful in generating ideas for this project. At an early stage in this work, Ian Markham, Dean and President of Virginia Theological Seminary, organized a faculty group to read and comment on my work in progress. I am thankful for his support, and for the concrete ways he furthers the writing and research of the VTS faculty. I thank too the faculty and practitioners who participated in this reading group, and who were diligent and thoughtful in their response to my work: Judy Fentress-Williams, Roger Ferlo, Ginger Gaines-Cirelli, Larry Golemon, Katherine Grieb, Judith McDaniel, Joyce Mercer, Timothy Sedgwick, and Kate Sonderegger. Other colleagues supported this work in its later stages, especially David Gortner, who generously read and commented on most of the manuscript. A grant from the Lilly Theological Research Grants program, a sabbatical grant from the Conant Fund, and a summer fellowship from the Wabash

Center for Teaching and Learning in Theology and Religion were crucial in enabling me to complete this volume.

The roots of this project go back a long way in my own life, but particularly to my interest in voice and embodiment—an interest sparked by my studies with Kristin Linklater, which inspired me to become a teacher of her approach to vocal training. I cannot overstate how crucial my work with her has been in shaping my vocation. I am grateful for her open-minded faith in me, for the ways she has helped me translate her work into my teaching context, and for the combination of encouragement and challenge that she has given me as her student, which has helped me grow into a teacher and scholar that I could never have been without her.

At Yale Divinity School I was blessed to find others who saw the relevance of this work and invited me to teach it with them there; I am thankful particularly to Peter Hawkins and Richard Ward. As a beginning preacher, I was fortunate to be an intern with James Bradley at St. John's Episcopal Church, Waterbury, Connecticut. Jim's preaching taught me much of what I know about this craft and discipline, and inspired me with the sense that preaching really can make a difference in this world. Professors at Yale, notably Marilyn McCord Adams, Ellen Davis, Serene Jones, and David Kelsey, taught me how to think theologically about the preaching task.

In the development of this book I have had the privilege and honor of speaking with some of the most creative, passionate, and dedicated preachers in the Episcopal Church: James Bradley, Mariann Edgar Budde, Susan Burns, Michael Curry, Ellen Davis, Zelda Kennedy, Martin Smith, Stephanie Spellers, Carol Wade, and Samuel Wells. Their commitment to the task of preaching, and the excellence with which they fulfill this ministry, inspires me with hope for the church of the twenty-first century. I thank them for the time they gave to this project, for their thoughtfulness and insight about their preaching, and for the gift that they are to the church and the world. Many people helped connect me with these preachers, especially Randolph Charles, Linda Clader, Ann Gillespie, Sarabeth Goodwin, Anthony Guillen, and David Schlafer.

I am also grateful to Heather Erickson, who generously shared with me her insights into the relationship between yoga and preaching, crucially shaping my understanding of the value of these two practices for each other. My students too have contributed to this project, both by their reading and response to drafts, and still more by their passion for preaching and experience of its challenges, which has spurred me to write this book, in hopes that it might help them fulfill this vital calling.

Anne Nesbet, Anne Ellestad, Ruth Hooke, Lisa Kimball, Rebecca Voelkel, and Will Waters are among the many who have assisted me in bringing this book to completion, through words of encouragement or talking through its ideas with me. Ginger Gaines-Cirelli in particular has been a vital conversation partner to me throughout my ministry; knowing that we share a vision for the church as a community that incorporates body, mind, and spirit in a holistic and incarnational expression of the faith has inspired me countless times to keep moving toward the realization of this goal.

There are two people to whom special thanks are due, without whom this project would not have been finished. Cynthia Shattuck has been an exemplary editor: patient yet appropriately demanding, honoring my voice yet shaping it with insight and sensitivity. I have learned a great deal from her, and am grateful for her mentoring of me. Finally, I offer grateful thanks to my partner Judy Adkins, whose constant faith in me, belief in this project, and willingness to sacrifice so as to help me complete it were indispensable throughout this process. She provides the nourishing love that has allowed this project in particular, and my vocation in general, to blossom, and so I gratefully dedicate this book to her.

—RUTHANNA B. HOOKE
February 2010

chapter one

Why Is It Frightening to Preach?

Then I said, "Ah, Lord GOD! Truly I do not know how to speak, for I am only a boy." But the LORD said to me, "Do not say, 'I am only a boy'; for you shall go to all to whom I send you. . . . I have put my words in your mouth."
(Jeremiah 1:6–9)

At the beginning of every semester I ask my students to choose a single word to describe how they feel to be in a preaching class. Some will choose the word "excited," but most pick words along the lines of "nervous," "terrified," or "petrified." Why are they afraid, and what are they afraid of? What is it about the act of preaching that makes it so terrifying? What makes preaching such a daunting task, so difficult to do well? Most of my students view preaching as a central part of their ministry, and they desperately want to do it well, which is one reason they find the task frightening. But why is it crucial that preaching be done well, and what would "doing it well" look like? What are the criteria of successful or effective or faithful (even the right adjective is hard to find) preaching?

The series of which this book is a part considers the ways that various practices of the church—stewardship, evangelism, reading the Bible—need to be transformed in order for the church to continue to be vital in the twenty-first century. These books respond to a sense of crisis in the church today, a crisis that challenges the church's life and practices in ways that it has not been challenged before. I am mindful of this crisis and these challenges too, yet in my experience the most serious difficulties that preachers face in undertaking the task of preaching are perennial ones. The task of preaching may be more demanding today for various reasons, and I will consider them in the course of this book; yet I believe the most daunting aspects of the preaching task are ones that have been with preachers, in one form or another, for centuries. The title of a recent book in the field of homiletics, *What's the Matter with Preaching Today?*, is a quotation from a Harry Emerson Fosdick essay of the same name written in 1928, which itself is commenting on a nineteenth-century diatribe about the sorry state of preaching at that time. This sequence suggests that there is always a sense that something is wrong with preaching; it is never being done as well as it should be.

We will see why the challenges of the preaching task are perennial ones if we examine the fear of preaching more closely. What makes preaching so terrifying? For one thing, preaching is a form of public speaking, itself something that intimidates many people. The phenomenon of stage fright is so consuming that it can drive even the most experienced actors away from the stage—even Lawrence Olivier is said to have suffered terribly from it later in his career. Many an actor or public speaker reports having a recurring nightmare of getting up to speak to others and losing the manuscript, having no clothes on, forgetting how to form words, speaking in a foreign language. Another variant on this nightmare involves getting lost on the way to the speaking engagement and never arriving at all. Clearly, there is much carryover between the fear of public speaking in general and the fear of preaching. However, I am always interested to note that the students who come to me with experience in other forms of public speaking usually find preaching just as frightening as those who have none. Former trial lawyers, salespeople, business men or women, and musicians will occasionally begin the preaching class claiming a greater confidence, but usually that self-assurance dissipates once they begin the practice of preaching. So what is it about preaching that makes it even more frightening than other forms of public speaking?

Another interesting fact about the fear of preaching is that it does not go away with practice, but rather tends to increase, or at least to hold steady, for a long time into one's preaching ministry. I have been preaching for over ten years, and the experience of my heart pounding and my legs locking as I get up to preach is still with me. It is similar to beginning to learn rock climbing, when I stood at the top of a cliff, attached to a rope, and had to launch myself over the side, trusting in the rope and in my climbing partners to hold me up over the abyss. The mind and body absolutely rebel against taking this step over the side into what feels like certain annihilation. The moment before I speak the first word of my sermon feels like this—like a launching over the abyss, into pure terror, while every fiber resists. This sense of risk is captured in preacher Barbara Brown Taylor's description of this same moment:

> Watching a preacher climb into the pulpit is a lot like watching a tightrope walker climb onto the platform as the drum roll begins. The first clears her throat and spreads out her notes; the second loosens his shoulders and stretches out one rosin-

soled foot to test the taut rope. Then both step out into the air, trusting everything they have done to prepare for this moment as they surrender themselves to it, counting now on something beyond themselves to help them do what they love and fear and most want to do. If they reach the other side without falling, it is skill but it is also grace—a benevolent God's decision to let these daredevils tread the high places where ordinary mortals have the good sense not to go.[1]

Frederick Buechner also evokes memorably the momentous silence just before the sermon begins, when he describes how the preacher "pulls the little cord that turns on the lectern light and deals out his note cards like a riverboat gambler. The stakes have never been higher."[2] The sense of risk and danger, the awareness of the momentousness of the occasion, the sense of high stakes and of the need to trust and surrender—all these are aspects of the fear of preaching, and as both these preachers seem to acknowledge, such fear does not necessarily go away with more experience. I am sorry to have to tell my students this, and yet, as I also tell them, I believe there is something *necessary* about the fear that accompanies preaching. I believe it is not meant to go away; rather, the challenge is to understand why preaching has to be scary, and also to understand how to work with the fear in a creative way, so that our preaching can be what it needs to be.

---

the challenge of proclamation

There are many reasons why preaching is a daunting and frightening undertaking. Let's consider, for starters, the role that preaching is meant to serve in the church: it is one of the primary ways that the Christian faith is taught, handed on, and commended to the church and the world.

A sermon is the moment in the worship service when the preacher takes the words of Scripture and the elements of the liturgy and seeks not only to explain them, but to make them relevant to the world today. In the sermon the preacher shows why we should care about the Bible verses that have been read and the traditional words and actions of the liturgy. Why does all of this matter to us today? The preacher's task is to bridge a gap between the texts and tradition of the church, and the world that we live in now, and to show why the Christian faith is the best way to make sense of this world and to give meaning to our lives. This is an exceptionally challenging task, because it is not always clear how a two-thousand-year-old text and centuries-old traditions ought to be what we turn to today in order to make meaning out of life. Moreover, the truths of these texts and traditions (that God is the all-powerful and all-loving Creator of the universe; that God has made an unalterable difference in the world through the life, death, and resurrection of Jesus Christ; that God is drawing us toward an eschatological fulfillment) can often be hard to proclaim in the face of suffering and evil. Perhaps the difficulty of proclaiming these truths is greater now than it has ever been, but this proclamation has always been a challenging one to make, and this is what preachers are charged with doing.

In order to make the truths of Scripture relevant to our times, preachers also must have the skill of being able to read the times accurately and insightfully, to interpret contemporary culture as well as biblical texts. This entails being able to put local events into a broader cultural context, to see the forest as well as the trees. If a marriage is in trouble, what are the larger cultural and economic forces pulling this relationship apart? What are the broader economic circumstances behind the closing of a local factory? Preaching well means being able to see and articulate these connections. E. M. Forster refers to this ability as "seeing life steadily and seeing it whole," and it is a trait that great leaders have. Barack Obama, for instance, demonstrates an ability to read the mood and the circumstances of these times, to analyze the maelstrom of current events in a larger historical context so as to make meaning of them. He showed this ability in analyzing his own life in his memoir *Dreams of My Father,* in which he wrote about his own local, personal experiences with race, belonging, place, community, and then was able to zoom out and reflect on these experiences in a much wider historical, cultural, and political perspective, making his own experiences meaningful even for those who had not shared them. He was able to bring the same gift for insightful cultural analysis to bear throughout his campaign, notably in his speech on race in America and in his inaugural address. In order to preach well, preachers too need this ability to understand and articulate the events, currents, and moods of these times, yet their task is still more challenging, since they must relate this reading of culture to the truths of the Christian faith.

God's Word and the preacher's words

In addition to the challenge of proclaiming the truths of Scripture in relationship to the events of today, the challenge of preaching also comes from the weighty theological claims that some strands of the Christian tradition make for preaching. The Protestant reformers, notably Martin Luther and John Calvin, argued that it was not enough to think of preaching as educating believers in the Christian faith or preparing them to receive the sacraments. For them preaching was itself sacramental and a means of grace. It was a moment when the Christian was presented with God's saving grace, and could accept or reject it; if accepted, this grace was a means of salvation.

This is what these theologians meant when they said that preaching was the Word of God—it was an encounter with God's very being, present in the sermon, offering judgment and mercy, offering salvation through grace alone, justifying the sinner. These reformers changed preaching from an educational tool to a transforming event in the life of a Christian.

> The word of God is living and active, sharper than any two-edged sword, piercing until it divides soul from spirit, joints from marrow; it is able to judge the thoughts and intentions of the heart. *(Hebrews 4:12)*

We may want to argue that these doctrines of preaching do not and need not influence us that much today. Episcopalians, for instance, may argue that they do not hold this high sacramental view of preaching. Our encounter with God occurs at the Eucharist, and thus preaching need not carry so much of the burden of being the principal place where the worshipper meets God. Still, to the extent that Anglicanism has a Protestant as well as Roman Catholic heritage, these theological claims about preaching are part of our formational beliefs about preaching too. They affect the ways that we think about preaching, what we think preaching is supposed to do. On some level Episcopal preachers too are influenced by the belief that God is speaking in a special way through preaching, that preaching is not just human speech like other human speech, but that something divine is happening in and through it. Such beliefs, lurking in the background or dimly sensed, add to the weight of the preaching event; these beliefs help to explain why we feel with Buechner that the stakes are very high when we preach, and why we feel afraid to do so.

For example, one experienced preacher acknowledges that even after twenty years in the ministry, there is a still a "moment of terror" as she enters into the preaching process. Her fear of preaching has several components. One kind of fear affects her in the preparation process, the fear that she will have nothing to say, or will somehow get it wrong. This is related to anxieties about public exposure; by temperament she is an introvert. There is also the fear that comes when she feels the challenge of the text upon her. She has come to realize that when in reading the Bible text ahead of time she says to herself, "Oh no, not that!" it is the exact area of the text that she needs to explore. Underlying this is the fear of God; since she believes that in preaching she is in God's presence, there is the terror of this encounter with God. There is fear in knowing that what she is talking about is supremely important, "the meaning at the heart of the world." In engaging such a crucial subject, there is the inevitable moment of thinking "Who, *me*?" and she has to push herself to the point of saying, "Yes, me," and trusting what God has given her. However, by the same token her years in the pulpit have taught her that the fear of preaching is an inevitable part of it; if she is not afraid, it would be a sign that she was not engaging deeply enough with the momentous task entrusted to her. Moving toward rather than away from the fear, she has come to see, is one of the sources of the power of her preaching. It is interesting, too, that all of her fear disappears by the time she is ready to preach, replaced by the excitement of telling the congregation what she has discovered.[3]

If preaching is part of God's self-revelation and a transforming encounter with God's own Word, what is the role of the preacher in this event? Preachers and theorists of preaching have struggled with this issue ever since Luther and Calvin first developed their doctrines of preaching. In the next chapter we will consider a few of the attempts to address this issue. But it is evident that much of the fear of preaching centers around questions of how the preacher's task and bearing relate to what *God* is doing in preaching. First, what is the event supposed to mean to and provide for others? Am I, as a preacher, obliged to facilitate a momentous and transforming encounter of the hearer with God? How can I fill such a tall order with my feeble words? Can a sinner like me be an effective minister of God's sacramental grace? Second, if it is true that preaching is an encounter with God, then the preacher must be the material that God is working with, just as God works with the bread and wine of the Eucharist to transform them. To preach is to feel God working with and through one's words and in one's very body, and to fall into God's hands in this way is a fearful thing, as the Letter to the Hebrews reminds us.

The Quakers got their name because they would begin to tremble when they felt the Spirit prompting them to speak in a meeting for worship. This experience of over-whelming awe and terror seizing the body was the sure sign that God wanted to speak through them. A similar sense of being overwhelmed with terror is also an experi-ence that preachers can have—and, I would argue, is like-wise a sign that God is very close, and is using the preacher's words, just as the "quaking" of a Quaker is a sign that the Spirit is speaking through her. Preaching is frightening, then, because it is a moment when God is working with and on the preacher intimately and intensely, and this sense of being in God's grip is at once exhilarating, comforting, and undeniably terrifying, as Scripture records again and again.

There is another dimension of the terror the preacher may feel as God works with her in the sermon, for this encounter with God is happening in front of a whole congregation. Most Christians who have a living relation-ship with God can recall times when their relationship with God was particularly tumultuous or perplexing, but for most believers, these harrowing times occur in the privacy of personal prayer or in the relative anonymity of the pew. For preachers, however, their relationship with God, in all its intimacy and challenge, is played out in front of the congregation, for all to see. That is the point, in a certain way—that the preacher's life with God is on display for others so that through the example of her struggles and joys with God those who hear her can find courage to venture deeper into their own relationship with God.

authenticity in preaching

These aspects of the fear of preaching point to yet another reason for the terror of preaching: preaching is invariably very personal. God may be revealed equally in preaching and in the sacraments, but the degree of the priest's personal exposure is much greater in preaching. The recitation of the Eucharistic Prayer can be and ought to be personally involving, but it is not personally revealing in the way that preaching is. This is so because of what preaching is, as I described earlier. Preaching is the moment when the preacher seeks to make the texts and traditions of the Christian faith relevant to the rest of us, to show why these texts and traditions ought to transform our lives. In order to do this, the preacher has to show why these traditions and texts are relevant to *him* and how they have transformed *his* life. If he is unable to do this, it is doubtful that he will be able to convince anyone else to believe in this transforming power. In a sense he is God's witness, on trial before a skeptical jury to try to show them that God's way is indeed the truth that should shape their lives. His whole life as a Christian is on the line. This requirement has many implications, one of them being that he has to show the congregation his heart and soul, explain why he believes in this God and what difference it has made to him. This is intimate self-disclosure, and hence terrifying.

There is a fierce debate in homiletical theory as to whether preaching should involve self-disclosure on the part of the preacher, but unfortunately the debate centers on the question of whether it is appropriate for the preacher to tell personal stories in a sermon. This focus muddies the debate, because it equates the telling of personal stories with genuine self-disclosure, and yet in my experience they are not the same thing. On the contrary, telling personal stories is not necessarily self-disclosure, and in fact may be a way of avoiding it. Telling personal stories can be a way of stoking the preacher's ego while side-stepping the greater vulnerability of true disclosure. Such stories can also be a way of *signaling* vulnerability but not actually *experiencing* it; such stories have a sentimental edge to them, as they make a show of vulnerability while actually keeping the preacher's deepest self hidden. So the appropriate question in this debate about self-disclosure in preaching is not about whether personal stories are allowable, but about whether such stories reveal or mask the preacher's true self. This is the key question, because this true self of the preacher is a necessary component of good preaching. Her personal involvement in the sermon is inherent to good preaching for the simple reason that it is as she displays how the Christian faith makes sense of her life that others can come to believe in it for themselves. Whether a preacher tells personal stories or not in a sermon, she is on display as a preacher, in a very intimate way. This fact, moreover, suggests that self-disclosure is inherent in *all* preaching, not just good preaching, because the preacher who stands apart from her words, suggesting thereby that God's presence has not made a difference in her life, also discloses much about herself.

What is asked of the preacher, fundamentally, is that he be present in his preaching. He is asked to show up, to claim and own his words and his beliefs, to inhabit them fully, and to offer them to the hearer. Yet this seemingly simple task is actually one of the most difficult things any human can do. Being present, showing up, is terrifying, as it is an experience of being naked in all one's humanity for the other to see. As the monk David Steindl-Rast puts it, "While we long for the wholeness and harmony that comes from being fully present to our moments, at the same time we are afraid of it." He goes on to ask, "Why is it that we are afraid to live in the now?" and then answers his own question: "We are afraid of becoming real."[4] The preacher is asked to undergo the frightening task of becoming real, fully present in the moment, so that God might become real and present through her. This demand for genuine self-disclosure and presence is one of the factors that makes preaching so terrifying, and is a central reason why my students who have other public speaking experience are surprised that preaching is so much harder. They find that they are on the line in a different way than in any other kind of public speaking. They are on display in a uniquely intimate way.

You cannot preach God's Word without putting
your own word, unprotected, on the line.
—Anna Carter Florence

Furthermore, the preacher is asked to expose her true self for others in the very act of explaining, defending, and passing on the Christian faith. She is in the paradoxical position of being in a role as religious leader and teacher and as a vessel for God's presence, yet at the same time she is also called upon to be herself fully. Many of my students feel a tension here between enacting the role (of priest, preacher, religious leader) while at the same time being their true selves, and this tension can cause anxiety. As they negotiate this tension, the quality they are seeking in their preaching is authenticity. The word "authenticity" carries connotations of credibility, trustworthiness, genuineness, being oneself or being true to oneself. The centrality of the quest for authenticity in contemporary times is itself interesting, as it suggests that many of us feel we are locked into roles that define us and yet do not reflect who we really are. This is true in a particular way with clergy and preachers, who are asked to step into a role as religious leaders, but also to be their true and often quite vulnerable selves in that role. This tension between self and role, the difficult quest for authenticity, is one of the chief factors that makes preaching so daunting for my students. My students know each other quite well, so when they listen to each other's sermons they will often make comments like, "That didn't sound like you, not like the person we know at the refectory dining table." Or a student will say, "I am having a hard time finding my voice in my preaching." Or, "I feel like an alien takes over my body when I get up there." These are all comments that suggest the distance between self and role—the difficulty of stepping into the role of preacher while also being one's real self. It is the elusive quality of "authenticity" that bridges this gap, but how do we find this authenticity amidst the high-stakes act of preaching, with all its levels of meaning that we have explored?

One priest I know has resolved this tension thoughtfully by finding that authenticity in preaching is a matter of becoming *more* oneself precisely *through* inhabiting the role of preacher. He describes his own experience of being in the pulpit, where he feels he is himself, yet in a heightened way. He is more conscious of himself yet less *self-conscious* than at other times—a state of hyperawareness that he likens to being in an airplane during take-off and landing. He is very aware of every noise; he feels every jolt; his heart comes into his throat; he sees every part of his surroundings. Similarly, in preaching he knows just what he is doing at each moment, yet he is focused on the act, rather than on himself. This state of acute awareness sounds much like fear, but he prefers to call it excitement, and for him that changes the experience completely.

He also explains the elusive quality of authenticity in preaching by likening it to the difference between "performing" and "acting." When a performer takes on a role, there is a perceptible gap between the person's self-hood and the role he is playing. With "acting," on the other hand, we as the audience feel the actor has *become* the role he is playing, with no perceptible gap between self and role. In the same way, a preacher is perceived as "inauthentic" when she takes on attributes that are not her own and becomes something she is not—but thinks she *should* be. The only way she can authentically inhabit the role of preacher is by trying *not* to play it. Here again we have a parallel with acting: the best way for an actor to play a drunk is by trying *not* to act drunk—because this is what a real drunk would do. Similarly, in preaching it is only by refusing to "act like a preacher" that can one successfully take on this role. Only when one does not *play* the preacher does one actually *become* the preacher. Once again, the paradoxical relationship between being both oneself and not-oneself in preaching is evident.

Authenticity depends not only on how the preacher takes up this role, but also how the content of her sermons relates to the quality of the rest of her life. It is only those who listen to a preacher week after week, furthermore, who can recognize authenticity in her preaching; they know that in the rest of the preacher's life she is the person she says she is. Authenticity is something that is within us, but it is also established relationally; that is, it needs to be recognized by others. For this reason, establishing authenticity in preaching takes time; some research shows that pastors need to stay in the same parish for many years for this quality to take root. Many clergy find that one of the benefits of remaining a long time in one parish is that members of the parish come to know them well enough to see that over time their words and deeds match.[5]

One preacher who is also a noted biblical scholar holds that the authenticity of her preaching comes in part from her willingness to submit herself to the scriptural text and let it challenge her ordinary ways of thinking and living. She believes that patience is necessary; it is important to slow down enough to ponder each word. This allows the text to challenge our entrenched positions and preconceptions, instead of simply reinforcing what we already believe and think we know. Often the key to interpreting a text is to ask oneself, "In what ways does this passage from the Bible challenge my ordinary ways of thinking about things?" This is a way of submitting ourselves to the text and its wisdom, becoming vulnerable to it and allowing it to address and change us. It is to read Scripture *ethically,* as the Word of God, with the power to challenge and invite us to repentance and transformation.[6]

It is through this process of deep engagement with our own religious experience, as well as learning how to negotiate the relationship between self and role, that a preacher eventually finds her authentic preaching voice. One preacher I interviewed, who is also a spiritual director who works with preachers, observed that it is impossible to arrive right away at this kind of authenticity in the preaching role. Along the way there will inevitably be posturing, clumsiness, artifice, and estrangement from oneself as the person takes on and grows into her role as a preacher. Often a person seeking to find her place in this role will lean into her strongest characteristics, and only in time will find the balance and integration that comes with knowing who she really is in this role. It is helpful to remember God's initiative during this process, to be reminded that God is struggling with the preacher to shape her into the preacher that God longs for her to be. God says to the beginning preacher, "How shall we be together in preaching?" As this relationship develops, there will be failure and flourishing, breakthrough and regression; thus it is important to remember that the development of an authentic preacher takes time.

---

questions of authority

This preacher also noted that there is a close relationship between authenticity and authority in preaching. He spoke glowingly of a parish priest who had both of these qualities. This priest gave his sermons in just the same tone of voice he used in everyday conversation, so there was a sense of seamlessness between his true self and his *persona* in the pulpit. Thus his congregation believed that he was fully living the truths he was transmitting. It was the truths themselves that were authoritative, and nothing about the preacher himself—except for the fact that he had appropriated them and knew them to be true. The authority of his preaching came from the fact that he had experienced the truths of which he spoke, he was expressing the things he was living, and so could be wholly himself in the preaching moment.[7]

As this example suggests, authority and authenticity are closely linked, in part because both are difficult qualities for the preacher to develop. Claiming true and life-giving authority as a preacher is probably even more difficult than finding authenticity in this task, and the challenge of exercising this authority is yet another source of the fear of preaching. Authority, like authenticity, is essentially a relational concept. Authority describes a relationship between A and B in the following way: authority consists of the idea that A's telling B to do X constitutes a good reason for B to do X. In other words, A's "say-so" has the power to shape B's thinking and behavior. It is evident that preaching aims to be authoritative speech in this way. The intent of preaching is that people will listen to it deeply enough that it will transform the ways they live their lives. For instance, the preacher commends the truths of Scripture and tradition not so that people will simply *learn* about these aspects of the faith, but so that they will shape their lives in accordance with these teachings. Likewise, the preacher becomes a vessel for God's presence not so that hearers will observe God's work as mere spectators, but so that they themselves will meet God and be transformed by the encounter. Preaching aims to be speech that has this kind of authority in people's lives.

Receive this Bible as a sign of the authority given you to preach the Word of God and to administer his holy Sacraments. Do not forget the trust committed to you as a priest of the Church of God. (The Ordination of a Priest, *The Book of Common Prayer 1979*).

But where does this authority come from, and how does a preacher claim it? On one level, the authority to preach is granted by the church when a person is ordained; in the ordination service in the *Book of Common Prayer*, the newly ordained priest is given a Bible "as a sign of the authority given to you to preach the Word of God." But it is one thing to be given this authority by the church as an institution, by virtue of one's office, and another thing to claim that authority personally and inwardly. And it is still a further step to be granted this authority by those who are listening. It is the feeling of this gap between institutionally granted authority on the one hand, and personally claimed and communally granted authority on the other, that leads to some of the fear that my students feel in preaching. They wonder, "Who am I to step into the pulpit and preach?" In my beginning class I do an exercise in which students step into the seminary chapel pulpit for the first time, an experience that often arouses doubts about whether they "belong" in this space, with all the authority that has been vested in it. This too is an experience of the tension between self and role, the challenge being how to find an authentic self when inhabiting an authoritative role.

During the elections of 2008 it was interesting to watch the candidates negotiate this tension between self and role, so as to exude both authenticity and authority. A key question throughout the campaign (as with any presidential campaign) was whether Barack Obama and John McCain were appropriately "presidential." The question was whether either candidate had the personal authority, the *gravitas,* to match the institutional authority he would be given as President—whether he would fit the role, in a sense. The temptation in any campaign is to allow this quest to fit the role to overwhelm one's own personal authenticity. Obama vowed at the outset of his campaign that he was going to "emerge intact" and there was a widespread sense that he succeeded in this—that he was convincingly presidential, yet was recognizably himself throughout, so that the voters felt that who they saw was who he truly was. He was able to find and to maintain authenticity in the midst of auditioning for and being granted a role. On the other hand, what may have sunk the campaign of John McCain, as well as those of Al Gore and John Kerry in earlier years, was the sense that they had compromised or suppressed some core part of themselves in order to get elected. They had let the demands of the role overwhelm who they really were, and thus their authenticity was lost. Although the role of preacher may not have as many demands and expectations laid upon it as that of President of the United States, the same potentially dangerous tension between authentic self and authoritative role characterizes the preacher's work also.

The challenge of finding and claiming personal authority in preaching is a perennial one, and yet perhaps this challenge is even harder to meet in contemporary times. Many homileticians have noted the waning of the traditional authority of preaching.[8] This has partly to do with a waning of the authority of preaching's sources, such as Scripture, and partly to do with different habits of communication. For instance, the lecture style of teaching has become increasingly outmoded, and is seen as hierarchical and static, yet this is the way preaching is usually done—as a monologue, with little to no congregational input. This style of communication may seem to many people to be old-fashioned, hierarchical, and difficult to treat as authoritative. These challenges make it more difficult than ever to claim the authority of preaching without feeling a sense of illegitimacy. It is interesting to note the increasingly widespread practice of preachers stepping down from the pulpit and speaking from the center aisle or walking around the sanctuary while preaching. This may be an attempt to step out of a more hierarchical style of authority, but it may also signal a preacher's discomfort with claiming *any* authority, or it may be a way that the preacher *pretends* to relinquish authority while actually holding on to it. In any case, this practice suggests some ambivalence with the idea that the preacher has any authority at all, or some confusion about what kind of authority he has and how to exercise it.

One more dimension to the fear of preaching is the loneliness of it. As I have described, preaching is the most public act the minister or priest performs in the congregation, and is inherently an act of self-disclosure, a display of one's personal faith for the benefit and transformation of the hearers. But the problem with this is that the preacher is doing this hard work of putting her life with God on the line, while those who listen are bystanders who are not at that moment expected to do this same difficult wrestling and engaging with God. Here again, the comparison with Quaker meeting is instructive. There, *every* participant is waiting upon the Spirit, with the expectation that the Spirit might call on any participant to speak and offer testimony. Every participant thus sits with the awesome and frightening sense of being in God's presence; everyone's life is on the line before God. But in the average church service this is not the case. The listener is a spectator, of whom nothing is demanded, who may safely judge the preacher from the sidelines. This means that the preacher is alone in his vulnerability before God and the people, a sense of exposure that can be isolating and frightening.

The loneliness of preaching is exacerbated by the culture in which we live, shaped through and through by consumerism—the idea that anything and everything in our lives is a commodity to be shopped for, bought, and sold. This attitude affects even the way people come to church—as consumers who are evaluating a community's life and a preacher's faith and performance to decide whether they are going to "buy" this particular "product." Even the common phrase "church shopping" indicates the attitude with which many people approach communities of faith and their leaders. Increasingly, even churches are talking about themselves as having a "brand" that needs to be built up and marketed to the public. Listening to sermons with this consumer mentality entails removing oneself from the event, such that listeners are waiting to see if the preacher has the skill to entice them in, rather than making themselves vulnerable to God's Word alongside the preacher. How can churches practice preaching in ways that invite listeners to be active participants in the sermon process and sermon event, so that they feel that in preaching they themselves are present and engaged with God, not watching from the sidelines?

The challenge and the terror of preaching arise from the "perfect storm" of the meeting of these various aspects of the preaching task. No wonder my students approach the task of preaching with fear and trembling! No wonder preaching is a task that is very hard to do well. The project of this book is to explore ways of thinking about and practicing preaching that help preachers rise to the challenge of this difficult and important work, as well as to suggest ways that congregations too can and should participate in this work. The goal is not to make the fear of preaching go away, but rather to turn unhealthy, anxious fear into the joyous awe that comes of being in God's presence and bearing God's Word into the world.

chapter two

"Is There a Word from the Lord?"

If I say, "I will not mention [the LORD], or speak any more in his name," then within me there is something like a burning fire shut up in my bones; I am weary with holding it in, and I cannot. (Jeremiah 20:9)

Of all the relationships that make up preaching, the one that exists between the preacher and God is probably the hardest to understand, causes the greatest trepidation, and poses the greatest challenge. Yet if we can understand how this relationship works in preaching, it will help us not only to understand better how our words and actions relate to what God is doing, but also to live in the preaching moment with greater openness and less fear. Of course, God's presence in our preaching is fundamentally a mystery, as is every other act of God, and one that we cannot fully pin down or describe. At the same time, it is helpful to say as much as we can about how we believe God is active in preaching, and how that relates to what we preachers are doing. But before we can do this, we need to tackle the fundamental theological claim that God is present and speaking through our sermons. Do we believe this?

I had a New Testament professor at divinity school who lectured brilliantly on the Bible. Normally they were just that—lectures. But when he lectured on Romans 8, and arrived at the statement that nothing "will be able to separate us from the love of God in Christ Jesus our Lord," we saw a perceptible change. He began speaking with greater conviction, he seemed close to tears, his voice took on a more rhythmic cadence—and one of my classmates leaned over to me and whispered, "He's preaching now!" We all put our pens down and listened; note-taking was no longer appropriate, because we were being addressed in a different way.

So what had happened in that moment? How did we all know that our professor had shifted from lecturing to preaching? In part, it was the palpable sense of his greater personal engagement in what he was saying, as well as the stylistic change in his speech. In part, though, it was a sense of "something more" that suffused the classroom, intangible but very real—the sense of there being some other power speaking through our professor, a power greater than himself that filled him and us at the same moment, giving his voice power and binding us all together into a shared experience.

It is this kind of experience that gives credibility to the theological claim that preaching is something more than ordinary speech. In this form of speech, it is not only a human being who speaks, but in some mysterious way, God is speaking as well. In fact, this example suggests what separates preaching from other human speech: it is precisely that speaking in which something beyond the human is at work. This claim has been put in various ways throughout the history of the church: that God is present in preaching, that preaching is the Word of God, that preaching is inspired speech, that preaching is a sacramental experience in which we meet God. Although all aspects of life can be occasions for encountering God, preaching is believed to be privileged, just as the sacraments are. This is why, in some churches, listeners approach the sermon not so much with the question, "What does the preacher have to say today?" but rather with the question, "Is there a Word from the Lord?"

But how do we justify this claim that God speaks? Where does this idea come from and how do we make sense of it? The Protestant reformers Martin Luther and John Calvin were the first to make a full-fledged theological defense of the idea that preaching is an event of encounter with God, on a par with the sacraments, but the conviction that God is present in preaching goes back to Scripture. The Hebrew prophets spoke not in their own name, but instead claimed they declared God's own words: "Thus says the Lord." They spoke not because they wanted to, but because God's Spirit filled them and compelled them to speak. The prophet Elijah prophesied when the Spirit came upon him; likewise, Isaiah proclaims, "The spirit of the Lord GOD is upon me, because the LORD has anointed me; he has sent me to bring good news to the oppressed" (Isa. 61:1).

The idea of preaching as speaking that is inspired and directed by the Spirit is carried over into the New Testament. In Jesus' own preaching, in the synagogue at Nazareth, he describes what he is doing in Isaiah's very words: "The Spirit of the Lord is upon me, because he has anointed me to bring good news to the poor" (Luke 4:18). Likewise, when Jesus commissions the disciples for their own preaching ministry, he tells them, "Do not worry beforehand about what you are to say; but say whatever is given you at that time, for it is not you who speak, but the Holy Spirit" (Mark 13:11).

The same pattern is evident in the first preaching of the disciples in the book of Acts. It is only after they receive the Holy Spirit at Pentecost that they are empowered to preach, as Peter immediately does. When the baffled onlookers believe he is drunk, Peter explains that in fact what they are seeing is the pouring out of the Spirit, as promised by the prophet Joel. Finally, Paul refers to his own preaching as Spirit-filled utterance, telling the Corinthians that he did not come preaching "words of wisdom, but with a demonstration of the Spirit and of power" (1 Cor. 2:4). Thus the experience of preaching is always described as one in which God, through the Holy Spirit, interacts with the preacher in a mysterious and powerful way that makes preaching something more than human utterance—it becomes the very voice of God.

Preaching can also be understood as an event in which God is present in a special way by likening it to the sacraments. The sacraments are "outward and visible signs of inward and invisible grace" (BCP 857), but the focus in recent sacramental theology has moved away "from thinking about the sacraments as objects that dispense grace to perceiving them as relational events, as personal encounters among God and people." This has meant a movement away from "abstract discussions of the principles involved in a given sacrament to increasing attention to liturgical action itself."[1] In other words, what is going on in the sacraments is best understood by examining what is going on in the liturgy as a whole. This wider focus suggests that the sacramental event, the encounter with God, takes place not only at the moment when the elements are consecrated or received, but throughout the entire liturgy. Thus preaching too, since it is embedded in the sacramental event of the liturgy, is a moment when God is present in a heightened way. In this sacramental description of preaching, the Spirit's work is central, just as it is in descriptions of proclamation in Scripture. It is the Holy Spirit who comes upon the elements of bread and wine and transforms them into Christ's Body and

Blood. Likewise, we could say that the Spirit comes upon the preacher and transforms his or her words into God's presence and Word.

If we believe that God speaks through human preaching, the key question preachers must wrestle with is what this means about what they are to do, say, and be in the preaching event. How are preachers to relate to God, and what God is doing? If we compare preaching to the sacraments, we see that this question of the preacher's role is complex. God's self-revelation is through the bread and wine of the Eucharist, but these elements do not have to "do" anything—they just have to be recognizably bread and wine. But preachers, unlike food, have free will, personalities, histories, family backgrounds, their own perspectives, and their own bodies. These factors can either help or get in the way of what God is doing and saying in preaching. Which aspects of the preacher's being and doing facilitate what God is doing, and which hinder it? This question is at the root of some of the fear and trembling associated with preaching, which arise because of uncertainty about the preacher's role. How can I be my true self while also being a conduit for God in the sermon?

One answer to this question is that the preacher's role is to be as transparent as possible and to "get out of the way," so that God can speak and act unhindered by the preacher's personality and perspective. After all, this argument goes, we are not God, and only God can reveal God—nothing we do can make this happen. A sermon ought to be about God, not about the preacher. I have heard of pulpits inscribed with the words from John's gospel, "Sir, we would see Jesus" (John 12:21); in other words, we would see Jesus and not the preacher, who should be humble and self-effacing, not drawing attention to herself. In terms of content, the sermon should be devoted to Scripture, which is what the preacher can do to keep the focus on God. For this same reason, attempts at self-disclosure do not belong in a sermon.

There is much to recommend this approach to understanding the preacher's role. Certainly the preacher cannot *make* God be present, and God needs to be the ultimate focus of the sermon. Moreover, this understanding of preaching helps keep it from becoming overbearing and authoritarian. Advocating the preacher's transparency is a way of limiting this ever-present tendency, the assumption being that the preacher who has "gotten out of the way" will preach in a humble rather than a domineering manner, pointing to God's authority rather than misusing her own.

> Christ, thou Word of God once spoken
> Speak thou in me.
> Christ, thou heart of God once broken
> Break thou in me.
> — *Kenneth Boulding*

However, there are both practical and theological problems with this description of the preacher's task. On a practical level, the preacher cannot actually make herself transparent; she is really, unavoidably, *there* in the pulpit, try as she might to "get out of the way." So in addition to seeing Jesus, her listeners see and hear her. The advice to be transparent is not helpful because it is impossible to follow. What is needed instead is some way of reflecting on *how* the preacher can keep the focus on God, and allow God to speak through her, even while she is still there and does not (cannot) go away.

The theological problem with this "transparency" argument is that it is not sufficiently incarnational. Christianity is a religion based on the Incarnation, the astonishing miracle that God became flesh and dwelt among us, in the person of Jesus of Nazareth. Christians believe that it is in this event that God is most fully revealed to us. God became present in the Incarnation by entering human history in this one particular person. No other god in any other religion has done this. This act of God tells us something important about God: that God's self is revealed to us *through* the fullness of being human. The humanity of Jesus of Nazareth did not "get out of the way"; Jesus did not become transparent, but was fully himself, a Palestinian man of the first century, and in this very humanity, God was revealed. What this means for preaching is that there too God speaks and becomes present by taking up, filling, blessing, and using our humanity, not by getting rid of it. Like Jesus, preachers have to be fully human in order for God to be made known in their preaching.

Being fully human in the pulpit does not mean telling personal stories or making oneself the focus, but something much deeper and more difficult. It is about bringing *all* of oneself—body, mind, and spirit—to the preaching task, to the encounter with God that takes place in preaching. Rather than seeking to "get out of the way" of God's Word, to become an empty channel or a transparent window, I experience my task as a preacher to be the challenge of coming as fully as possible into myself, into my body, my voice, and my presence in the room with a group of listeners. This is an extraordinarily difficult task in itself, as anyone knows who attempts to do it. It requires discipline, courage, and above all, the willingness to be vulnerable. The paradox of this event is that it is only when I can do this, can be where I am, doing what I am doing and saying what I am saying, that I become transparent, such that something larger than I am can speak through me. Then God takes my words and makes of them something much holier than I can do by myself, but my availability is part of what makes this possible.

To be present like this is to feel the contrast between our vulnerability and God's power, as we see when we consider preaching in the Bible. We are told that when the Spirit came upon the Hebrew prophets, they often hesitated and drew back, insisting that they were unworthy or incapable of delivering the message God had given them. Moses said, "Who am I that I should go to Pharaoh?" (Exod. 3:11), and when God's call came to Jeremiah, he said, "Truly I do not know how to speak, for I am only a boy" (Jer. 1:6). In the gospels, Jesus has to reassure the disciples that the Spirit will give power to their utterance in their hour of need: "Do not worry about how you are to speak or what you are to say, . . . for it is not you who speak, but the Spirit of your Father speaking through you" (Matt. 10:19–20). Paul explores this paradox most fully when he *deliberately* eschews a powerful preaching *persona,* so that the power of his utterance would most definitely be ascribed to the Holy Spirit rather than to him: "I came to you in weakness and in fear and in much trembling, . . . so that your faith might rest not on human wisdom but on the power of God" (1 Cor. 2:3, 5). It is through Paul's vulnerability, through the "foolishness" of his proclamation, that the Spirit's power is revealed.

> Lord, how can man preach thy eternal word?
> He is a brittle crazy glass:
> Yet in thy temple thou dost him afford
> This glorious and transcendent place,
> To be a window, through thy grace.
> — *George Herbert, "The Windows"*

What it means to be fully human in preaching is fundamentally about a quality of presence that communicates itself beyond any particular words. Presence is difficult to describe, but we know it when we see it. It has to do with a person's bearing, his way of being. When a preacher is fully present, he is at one with his words, fully connected to what he is saying, and experiencing his words as he speaks them. This kind of presence is the most desirable quality to be sought in preaching, but it is difficult to attain, in part because we believe that if we are speaking for God we cannot speak from ourselves. However, true presence in preaching is the experience of speaking for God *while* being fully oneself, and not pretending to be God or anyone else. It is offering my own particular life as the window through which the divine light is refracted. Being present in this way in the preaching encounter says something about God—in, with, under, and beyond any words I speak.

This kind of presence also affects how preachers relate to their hearers. Much of the fear of preaching stems from the sense of separation between preachers and hearers: as one who is meant to speak for God, the preacher is set apart and on display, placed literally on a pedestal, while the congregation observes from a safe distance. The kind of presence I am recommending is a way of removing some of this feeling of distance and separation. It is true that God is speaking through the preacher's words, but only to the degree that she takes the risk of exposing herself in her full humanity, vulnerable and open to those who listen. This sense of a shared humanity alleviates the feeling of disconnection from hearers and invites the congregation to be fully present also. When a preacher can be present as the person she truly is, this gives permission to those who are listening to do the same. This mutuality can remove some of the fear and isolation a preacher feels—he is not alone, for his congregation is with him in the adventure of preaching.

performance as a metaphor for preaching

In order to better understand this relationship between God and the preacher, and also to *practice* it, it is helpful to investigate the metaphor of performance. It is notable that theologians have turned to the metaphor of performance to describe the human relationship to the divine, as well as the believer's relationship to his faith. For instance, Archbishop Rowan Williams employs the metaphor of performance to describe the relationship between the eternal Son of God (the second person of the Trinity) and the human Jesus of Nazareth. He argues that the metaphor of performance is a powerful one for describing this relationship between Jesus Christ's divinity and his humanity. Using the example of musical performance, Williams notes that the musician uses every ounce of her skill and concentration to bring to life the work of the composer. She remains herself, and yet is completely taken up by the work and vision and even the selfhood of another:

> Here is someone who is completely themselves, free and independent, and yet for this time the whole of their being, their life, their freedom, their skill, is taken up with this mysterious, different thing that is the work to be brought to life. The vision and imagination of another person, the composer, has to come through—not displacing the human particularity of the performer but "saturating" that performer's being for the time of the performance.[2]

Jesus, Williams argues, is a performer in this way; he is performing God's love and God's purpose, and performs them perfectly, "yet he is never other than himself, with all that makes him distinctly human taken up with this creative work." His is "a human will and a human life whose power and joy is the performance of who God is and what God wants, the performance of the Word of God."[3] As a performer of God's Word, Jesus is "saturated" through and through with God's life, and yet, paradoxically, his humanity is most fully real in that performance.

Thus Jesus of Nazareth becomes most himself by performing God most fully.

This theological understanding of performance is helpful for preachers, for just as Jesus brings the fullness of his humanity to performing the Word of God, so too the preacher must bring her own humanity to the event in order for it to be revelatory and authoritative. Williams argues that in Jesus of Nazareth's "performance" of the Son of God, Jesus "is never other than himself, with all that makes him distinctly human taken up with this creative work."[4] It is precisely in being his fully human self that Jesus is "saturated" by God, and in this saturation Jesus becomes the fullness of his human self. Williams's theology of performance shows how divinity and humanity can be related in the event of preaching so that the human is honored rather than erased. The metaphor of performance suggests that it is *necessary* for the preacher to bring herself fully to the preaching event, and only thus is God also fully present.

At the same time, this idea of "performance" as a useful metaphor for a preacher's practice requires some fine-tuning, since the term "performance" has negative connotations when used of preaching and liturgy. Certainly there is something wrong with both preaching and liturgy if it feels like "acting"; if we come away from a sermon or liturgy saying it felt like a performance, this is a negative judgment. Understood this way, "performance" means deception, something artificial, a lie, something that covers up the truth rather than revealing it. If we look at the root meaning of the word "perform," however, a different picture emerges: "per-form" means to "fully form"—to carry a form through to completion.[5] It refers to a carefully structured and crafted action that allows a deeper truth to emerge than what we might ordinarily experience. Liturgy is this kind of performance. Performance in this sense is not about hiding truth but revealing it; it is not a deception, but an art form that allows for deeper truth-telling.

There are at least four kinds of meaning attached to the term "performance." First, performance is a public display of particular skills, such as a musical recital. Second, performance entails a certain distance between self and behavior, as for instance the distance between an actor and the role this actor plays on stage according to a script. Third, a performance has symbolic potential— ordinary actions are merely carried out, but actions are *performed* in order to convey a particular meaning. Finally, a performance is capable of being measured and judged; we speak of the "performance" of one car compared to another, a Toyota as opposed to a Dodge. The fact that the decision about the success of the performance rests with an outside authority, furthermore, highlights the element of display inherent in performance; it is always done *for* someone other than the performer. This final character- istic points to an element of performance that is inherent in all these meanings, what performance theorists call the "consciousness of doubleness, according to which the actual execution of an action is placed in mental compar- ison with a potential, an ideal, or a remembered original model of that action."[6] This doubleness often leads to the sense of a gap between ideal and execution—for instance, when a pianist plays a sonata, we ask how close he comes to realizing the full potential of that piece.

These elements of performance highlight several of the challenging aspects of preaching. The sense of "double- ness" exists in various ways in preaching, and contributes to its difficulty. It is found in the gap between who the preacher is and what she is attempting to communicate— that sometimes painful awareness of a distance between the flawed and finite person she is, and the God whose Word she is supposed to proclaim. We can also recognize this gap in terms of the distance between the private self and public role in preaching. The idea of performance also captures the notion of being lonely and on display, as a preacher explores the often challenging relationship between herself and the text, herself and God, in front of a whole congregation, which judges the success of her effort as spectators rather than participants. Finally, performance points to the symbolic nature of the very act of preaching itself—what is communicated simply in the way that preaching is carried out, far beyond the words the preacher utters. Thus, the metaphor of performance draws attention to several aspects of the preaching task that make preachers most uneasy and fearful. By exploring how performers work with these tensions, preachers too can find ways to negotiate the complex relationships and dynamics of the preaching event.

An actor, like a preacher, is always negotiating the relationship between himself, the character he is playing, and the audience who is watching. Sometimes a performer experiences a gap in these relationships, a distance between himself and his character, or himself and his audience, and much of learning how to perform is learning how to negotiate or close this gap. To embody a character requires the actor to bring the fullness of his thought, feeling, and life experience to the role—everything he is. That is the only way that he can become a channel for the character. He is the vehicle to the revelation of something beyond himself, but he still needs to be there in order for this to happen, using his life experience as the raw material through which he can reveal the character authentically. In a paradoxical way, the actor is both himself and not himself when on stage. In good acting there is a meeting between the truth of the actor and the truth of the character, so that both parties are illuminated fully. In bad acting this meeting does not happen; either the actor's personality overshadows the part or there is a sense that the actor is not able to fill the role with meaning.

The idea and the practice of performance is also helpful for preachers because it emphasizes that preaching is not only a periodic event in the life of a priest or minister, but a way of life. Scholar Nicholas Lash argues that Scripture only comes to life when it is "performed," that is, embodied in the lives of Christians.[7] Theologian Stanley Hauerwas develops this idea in arguing that the Christian life is primarily neither subjective experience nor objective knowledge, but a performance, a set of actions.[8] He gravitates to the term "performance," because he argues that it provides a place for human creativity and initiative yet takes place within a set of rules provided by Christian tradition. He prefers the term "performance" to "action" in part because the former conveys this idea of behavior that attempts to embody a given tradition.

Be patterns, be examples in all countries, places, islands, nations, wherever you come; that your carriage and life may preach among all sorts of people, and to them. Then you will come to walk cheerfully over the world, answering to that of God in every one; whereby in them ye may be a blessing, and make the witness of God in them to bless you.
— *George Fox (1656)*

For Hauerwas, the concept of performance also high-lights the quality of display, of something that is done primarily for others. He points out that the intelligibility and persuasiveness of the faith depend not on abstract criteria but on convincing performances of the faith in individual believers' lives. A credible performance of the faith on the part of a Christian persuades others to believe in its truth. Inherent in this idea is the notion that Christian faith is not simply lived in private, but also in public—it is on display to others in order to change them. Not only do we persuade others, moreover, we also persuade ourselves; we become most ourselves through entering a particular role, namely the role of being a Christian.

Hauerwas uses the concept of performance much as he and other ethicists have used the idea of *practices* in other contexts to describe a pattern of meaningful actions that shape people in certain ways. Hauerwas focuses on practices to emphasize that Christians are shaped as much by what they do repeatedly over time as by what they believe. This understanding of practices is helpful in suggesting how the practice of preaching, as it unfolds over a lifetime, transforms preachers into their authentic selves. However, the language of performance is even more useful than that of practices to describe preaching, since it illuminates the peculiar kind of Christian practice that preaching is. To call preaching a performance highlights the fact that it is a practice with a particularly acute tension between the practicing self and the faith that is practiced. This heightened tension is salutary, in that it compels the preacher to learn how to be her true self in the preaching event. Preaching is performance because it demands the best of us, even as it requires us to rely on God's grace. All Christian practices are, in one way or another, on display to others, and this display is what others evaluate in order to decide if they want to be Christians also. But preaching is a practice that is more "on display" than almost any other Christian practice. The idea of performance shows how we can negotiate these tensions, and calls us to commit our full selves, and our whole lives, to the performance of our faith. Preaching is merely one part of this total performance.

the body in preaching

Both the doctrine of the Incarnation and the metaphor of performance urge us to be present in our full humanity when we preach. This means being present in body as well as in mind and spirit. The term "embodiment" has a range of meanings, and draws our attention to various aspects of the preaching event. The most fundamental of these, and strangely enough one of the most overlooked, is the question of what is happening in the bodies of both preachers and listeners. When we ask what is the *physical* experience of preaching, several questions come to mind:

- How are the bodies of preachers and hearers aligned?

- How is breath traveling (or not traveling) through, between, and among these bodies?

- How are vocal vibrations being produced and received in the bodies of preachers and listeners?

- How do physical movements and gestures and postures—on the part of both preachers and listeners—contribute to the communication?

- How are these bodies experiencing either tension or relaxation in the speaking and hearing experience?

- How are they positioned in relation to each other and to the worship space?

- How are these bodies attired?

These are concrete and fundamental questions and yet we tend to overlook them when we think about preaching. When we speak of bringing all of ourselves to the preaching event, we assume it means bringing the totality of our history, our emotions, our mental faculties, our perspective on the world—but not our bodies. It is as though we do not think of our bodies as truly belonging to us, or, more profoundly, *being* us. We tend to think of ourselves as spirits who possess bodies, or worse, spirits locked in bodies. We are inclined either to ignore the body or to reject it or strive to control it, but we do not really integrate our bodies into the fullness of who we are. This is problematic in any activity in which we are called upon to be fully present, but especially so in preaching because it is such a physical activity. Our bodies are at the very center of what we are doing; we are standing in front of others, with our bodies on display, and we are using our voices and bodies to communicate. Words and experiences are filtered through our physical selves.

The very term "embodiment" suggests a process that we must continually work on. We must become *em-bodied*, come into our bodies, rather than being *dis-em-bodied*, as we often are in our daily lives. To become an embodied preacher takes work; it is a task that needs to be continually repeated, since there are powerful forces at work in both secular culture and the Christian tradition that tend to separate our bodies from our spirits. There are specific tools and techniques that can help us undertake this process of embodiment. Many of the tools that I have found most helpful come from the world of acting and the performing arts, since actors and performers give considerable attention to training their voices and bodies to communicate effectively.

Performance theory and practices emphasize that bringing our whole selves to the preaching event means bringing our bodies as well as our minds and spirits. Much of an actor's education involves training the body and the voice, because becoming fully present so that one can embody a character in a play is a physical activity as well as a mental and spiritual one. Our bodies can actually teach us *how* to be present, and to be present in a way that is truly open to God and to our hearers. In other words, we can learn how to be more fully present through certain physical practices—of alignment, breathing, and the natural use of the voice. Through these performance practices, we discover in our very bodies what it feels like to be both fully present and, in a mysterious way, fully open for God to become present through us. What seems like a paradox on an intellectual level becomes comprehensible and practicable on a physical level. (We will explore some of these specific performance practices in chapter 4.)

In addition to focusing our attention on the physical experience of the preacher, the term "embodiment" also allows us to think more deeply about the physical experience of those who listen to preaching. How is breath traveling through the bodies before us? Are they sitting up straight, leaning, or slumping? Are they making noise, fidgeting, or whispering? Do they seem tense and rigid, or relaxed and attentive? These are questions seldom asked about preaching, for two reasons. First of all, we tend to think of preaching not as a dialogue, but as a monologue. Unless the preacher is speaking to an empty church, however, those listening are inevitably participating in the communication in some way. Second, just as we tend to forget that preaching is an embodied activity, taking place in the body of the preacher, we also overlook the fact that preaching is an embodied activity for the listeners as well. Something is happening in their bodies during the sermon, and it is useful to know what.

In order to answer these questions, it is necessary to consider a further dimension of the sermon's embodiment: not only what is happening within the bodies of preacher and hearers, but how these bodies are interacting with each other:

   ◆ How are the bodies of the listeners positioned in
   relation to each other, to the preacher, and to the
   worship space as a whole?

- What does it mean that the preacher is often physically higher than the congregation, and enclosed in a small walled enclosure that hides part or most of his body?

- How are the listeners' bodies attired, compared to the attire of the preacher? What does it mean that the preacher often wears robes that obscure her body?

- What are the social backgrounds of listeners and preacher—their gender, race, class, sexual orientation?

In sum, the term "embodiment" draws our attention to all the material aspects of the preaching event: who is speaking, who is listening, how the event is staged, and what props, sets, and costumes are used. In other words, something is being communicated in preaching even before and beyond any words that are spoken. Something is being conveyed in the mere fact of who is speaking and who is listening, as well as in the staging of the event. As Charles Campbell points out, there is a *that* of preaching even before there is a *what* of preaching; *how* we execute the task of preaching says something, even beyond the particularity of the words that are spoken.[9] In order to know just what our sermons are communicating, we need to examine what is being conveyed in the *that* of preaching, as well as in the *what*.

There is certainly a critical edge to these questions, which we could express in theological terms. The fundamental question underlying these questions about the material dimensions of preaching (how preaching is embodied) is whether the *that* of preaching is congruent with what we believe about God, Jesus Christ, the church, and humankind:

- Does the relationship between preacher and hearers reflect what we believe about how we are related to each other in the body of Christ?

* Does the staging of the event reflect what we believe about how God relates to us?

* Does the fact that, in most instances, only a few in the congregation are allowed to preach reflect how we believe God speaks to us?

If we answer "no" to these questions, then our task is to transform the *that* of preaching—what the event of preaching communicates beyond any words we speak—so that it more truly expresses or embodies what we believe. This critical questioning is one benefit of focusing on the embodiment of sermons.

For instance, listeners' bodies might not be truly awake and listening actively. Breath may not be traveling freely through their bodies to enable them to receive what the preacher is saying. If we ask why this is so, this may lead us to the physical layout of the church: Are the members of the congregation placed in rows where they cannot see each other? Is the preacher above and beyond them, making them passive spectators? Focusing on questions like these helps us to see how the practice of preaching might not be accurately reflecting what we believe, and hence may lead to change.

In the broader and more metaphorical sense, the term "embodiment" refers not only to the physical experience of preacher and hearers and to the material set-up of the preaching event, but to the way that our words as preachers cohere with the whole of our lives. Embodied communication requires not only the integration of body, mind, and spirit, but also integration between what we say and how we live. When we say that a preacher fully embodies his words, we mean not only that there is a sense that the words are filled with meaning and that the words are being communicated through his whole body; we also mean that we sense that the preacher lives the truth of which he speaks. His whole life bears witness to his words, and this is why his sermons feel fully embodied. Here again, this witness is conveyed in the *that* of the preacher's bearing and presence, before and beyond his specific words, the *what* of the sermon. The focus on embodiment points to the importance of personal integrity: the preacher's life matches his proclamation.

---

breath as relationship in preaching

How does this emphasis on embodiment help address the challenges of preaching we explored in chapter 1? One of the major challenges is the difficulty of knowing how our presence and actions in preaching relate to God's presence and action. If we are not to be transparent in preaching, not supposed to "get out of the way" but instead to bring all of ourselves to the preaching task, how do we do it? How do we experience the relationship between God and ourselves as preachers? How does being present allow for God to speak and act through the preacher?

The focus on the body can give us concrete information in answer to these questions, for we can experience this relationship between God and ourselves in our bodies, and especially in the experience of breathing. If a person is truly breathing from the diaphragm, then she is truly present; to withhold her breath is to withhold her presence. Learning how to breathe correctly takes practice: she must stand in alignment, be aware of her body, and allow her breathing muscles to relax sufficiently that the diaphragm and lungs can expand and contract freely. However, once she achieves this state of relaxation, alignment, and openness, she merely has to *allow* the breath to enter and leave her. She does not control its movement, but is receptive to its rhythm. In a sense, she is breathed; although she prepares for it actively, breathing itself is a passive event.

The way in which my presence makes God's presence possible is analogous to the way free breathing happens. I must bring myself into the room, which I do through certain practices—for instance, by the way that I stand and, at a deeper level, by my will to be present, to be vulnerable. It is only after I undertake these steps that it is possible for the breath to move through me, for God to speak through me. While the final event of God's speaking through me is not mine to initiate, the stages leading up to this event require my participation and my presence. By contrast, when I pretend I am not there, when I try to hide myself while I am preaching, I make it impossible for anything to happen through me. God the Holy Spirit breathes through me not when I have become empty, but in the very fullness of my humanity, my breath, body, and voice.

> The English word "spiritual" finds its root in the Latin *spiritus,* which means both "breath" and "spirit." Equivalent words in Hebrew and in Greek are *ruach* and *pneuma.* Both breath and spirit bring us to life, or "inspire" us. And there, in all its simplicity and depth, we find the connection between prayer and the life-giving breath of God. Just as breath constantly renews the body, filling the lungs with oxygen and emptying the lungs of carbon dioxide, so also our prayer constantly opens us to God's life within us and helps us empty ourselves of those things that are alien to fullness of life. —*Nancy Roth*

Breath is also the way we open ourselves to those who are hearing us, rather than being closed off from each other. Breath is the connection between us. In one very difficult but transforming acting exercise the actor stands opposite a partner and simply looks at him and breathes—in a sense, breathing him in. If the two partners can relax into the experience, it is possible for them to bring their breath into a common rhythm, so that they are breathing together. This is a powerful experience of connection to the other. This sense of a shared breath, between speaker and hearer, again shifts the focus from the *what* of preaching to its *that*; before and beyond any words spoken, there is an exchange of breath between speaker and hearer that is communicating something important.

To help my students experience this, I ask them simply to take a moment in the pulpit to breathe before they start preaching. This breath allows for the listener to breathe also, and perhaps even for preacher and hearer to attune their breath to each other. It is very likely that this attunement is happening unconsciously anyway; I have noticed that when I am listening to sermons and I begin to feel a bit short of breath, it is because the preacher is not breathing and I am picking up on her breathlessness. Conversely, if the preacher can establish a free and relaxed breath from the outset, this can help the hearer breathe in this way also. As we have said earlier, this free breath is the foundation of the mutual presence of preacher and hearer that allows for God's presence to be most fully felt.

To think of this breathing experience in theological and sacramental terms, we could say that what is happening when the preacher breathes is that the Holy Spirit, the divine breath, is bringing God's presence into his very body, and as the listeners breathe with him, the Spirit enters their bodies as well. This moment of the Spirit sanctifying the human body is parallel to the way that the Spirit sanctifies the bread and wine in the consecration of the elements in the Eucharist. The preaching moment becomes sacramental through the presence of the Spirit in the bodies of the one who preaches and those who listen. Extending this metaphor even further, one could say that, just as the bread of the Eucharist is taken, blessed, broken, and shared with the congregation, so likewise the preacher is taken and blessed, in the sense that all of his life, his distinctiveness, his "skill and joy," as Rowan

Williams puts it, are offered in service to God's Word. He is broken—a preacher must become profoundly vulnerable and even wounded, so that the holy can be manifest through him. Finally, the preacher is shared, in the sense that there is a communion of souls that takes place when preaching becomes sacramental—a sense that preacher and hearers have drawn close to each other, even as the Spirit has drawn close to each of them. It is through this series of actions, this kind of performance, that the holy is made manifest so that all may partake.

Exploring the preacher's presence in the sermon as a matter of embodiment helps address in concrete ways the challenges of preaching. Through the physical experience of breathing, we can understand how our bodies and wills are related to God in ways that honor both the human and the divine participants in preaching. Through the breath, and the experience of embodied speaking, we can establish a connection with our congregation that involves them as participants rather than spectators, and alleviates the isolation that often accompanies preaching. In other words, in our physical experience we can make creative the tensive relationships that cause fear in preaching: between ourselves and God, ourselves and our hearers, ourselves and Scripture, and ourselves and our role. While the fear of preaching never fully goes away—and never should—as we become grounded and alive in our bodies, this fear is transformed from paralyzing terror to awe and excitement.

chapter three

Profiles of Preachers

Who dares, who can, preach, knowing what preaching is?
—Karl Barth

The task of this chapter is to examine the practices and philosophies of a small number of preachers in the Episcopal Church in order to discover what gives them a certain quality of presence and authority in the exercise of their craft. As we ponder what we can learn from them it is clear that, as with any group of artists, what they do cannot be strictly copied. Each person finds his or her own way to fulfill the calling of preacher, and one person's practices may not work well for others. However, the strengths of these preachers, especially their integrity, commitment to the preaching task, and passionate conviction about what they are saying, can lead us to some vital questions about the art of preaching:

• What tools can preachers use to help them engage more deeply and powerfully in their relationships with Scripture, God, congregation, and self?

* How can preachers make themselves more open to God and the congregation so that preaching becomes a conversation among these three parties?

* What practices can help preachers discover the appropriate balance between self and role, between private self and public *persona*?

The preachers I have interviewed for this chapter represent a fairly diverse cross-section of the Episcopal Church in terms of race, gender, geographical location, and types of congregations served. Some of them are well-known preachers, others less so. Despite these differences, all of these preachers do have several things in common. I would consider all of them to be outstanding preachers, although their preaching styles vary considerably. They are experienced preachers, since my conviction is that preaching is a practice that one learns over a long period of time. They take the preaching task seriously as a central part of their ministries, and take time to reflect on it. Most importantly, in my opinion all of them manifest in their preaching those elusive qualities of authenticity and authority that are so vital in preaching that matters. Their preaching has the ring of truth, and when I hear it, it feels important to listen, and to listen well.

In these interviews I began with general questions about how these preachers understand their preaching ministry, what they believe they are doing when they preach, what they understand to be the purpose of their preaching, why preaching is an important and even unique practice in the life of the church. Then I asked how they are able to find both authority and authenticity in their preaching, and how these two qualities might be related to each other. We went on to talk about the ways that they understand and inhabit the various relationships involved in preaching, and how their ways of being in these relationships is related to the authority and authenticity of their preaching. Finally, I asked what it meant to them to understand and undertake preaching as an embodied event—what role their bodies play either in the preparation or delivery of sermons.

---

preaching as theocentric discourse

Martin Smith, who is senior associate rector at St. Columba's Parish in Washington, D.C., is a well-known preacher, writer, spiritual director, and retreat leader. His preaching is much influenced by his many years as a brother in the Society of St. John the Evangelist, a religious order for men in the Episcopal Church. At St. Columba's he is responsible for adult education and formation, as well as regular preaching. His sermons are intellectually rigorous and demanding, yet emotionally engaging as well, involving a compelling mixture of serious wrestling with the biblical text, and keen psychological insight into the human condition.

Smith describes preaching as "theocentric discourse"— that daring and rare event in the church in which God is spoken of as the subject rather than the object of the sentence. Preaching is about going out on a limb to claim that God is, God does, God beckons, God grieves, and so on. Preaching is "dramatically serious" when a preacher is prepared to go out on this limb, resisting the tendency to make the church about everything else other than God— a social club, a political organization, a "charming community." This pressure can become so strong that churchgoers are actually offended when preaching dwells too much on God or on Jesus Christ. Such listeners find the focus on God unnerving because it entails a loss of ownership of the church, the recognition that the church belongs to God rather than to human beings. However, Smith insists that preaching is not important unless God is the subject of its sentences; without this, it is an outmoded form of the entertainment industry.

That is why Smith's desire in preaching is to alert people to God as a presence of initiative, reaching for and touching them. He hopes that people come away from a sermon thinking, "Is this how God wants to be in my life?" This ought to be the first stage of reflection, rather than "Is this how *I* want God to be in my life?" This second question might come later, but the first level of awareness is of God's presence and action. Ways of describing this initial beckoning by God vary, but Smith wants particularly to expand descriptions of this experience beyond the traditional notion that God is "speaking" to me. He suggests that we might want to draw on all the senses at our disposal, including our sense of touch. Hence, we might say that God touches or stirs me in a sermon; such language captures the inchoate way that people are often made aware of God in a sermon more accurately than the traditional language of hearing God's Word.

One of Smith's principal strategies for helping hearers encounter God in a sermon is to bring them to a place of discomfort and ambivalence. Many Christians believe that conflict is bad and needs to be resolved as quickly as possible; hence the rhetoric of assuaging conflict and smoothing it over. However, Smith maintains that conflict is part of our vitality as well as inevitable in our lives; we live in a state of tension between our deepest desires and our need to suppress or sabotage those desires. We also live in a state of ambivalence in our relationship to God, yet God's presence is disclosed in the very midst of this condition. This is an understanding of God's presence that is linked to Smith's conviction that God is indwelling and embodied, not a remote figure judging and observing us from on high. Hence one major purpose of the sermon is to awaken people to their own inner dis-ease, their ambivalence toward their own desires. The experience

Smith hopes to create in sermons includes that of being surprised or caught off-guard, so that people will find themselves saying, "Did I really hear the preacher say that? I never knew you could say that in church, but in fact it describes how I feel. I didn't know you could be this honest about my fear and desire, yet this is really what I experience."

To prepare sermons that accomplish this experience of dis-ease requires the preacher's own entry into this territory of ambivalence and conflict. For Smith, this means bringing his body into conversation with the biblical text. His first step is a brief foray into the text, which involves reading it and then stowing it away, so it can be worked on by the psyche. He does not approach the text directly at this time, but rather allows it to work on him "underground." During this phase ideas might surface as he is taking a walk, ironing, or doing some other physical activity, a sign that this unconscious process of working on the text is going on. Then comes direct engagement with the text, what Smith describes as "hunkering down," which involves sitting on a prayer stool for one or two sessions of forty-five minutes each. It is important to place the body in a certain position in order to create a state of spiritual readiness. These sessions are meditative, an "invitation for the temperature to rise," in which he seeks a state of emotional availability to the text and to God, hoping to "bring the sermon to a boil." This part of the preparation process Smith calls "hot thinking," and is a physical as well as mental experience, producing rising tension, a heating up of the emotional tone of his reflections, a speeding up of the reflective brain, an elevated heart rate, a raising of the pitch of his feeling and thinking, which eventually leads to a "cascade of insights" that are then going to be laid out in the sermon. It is during this part of the process that most of the work of birthing the sermon happens.

For Smith, this experience is akin to inspiration, yet he does not view it as something God is doing *to* him as though he, the preacher, were merely passive, an empty vessel. That is untrue to our experience. Rather, Smith thinks of the preacher as a co-creator with God. A kind of "sacramental chemistry" comes into play, which requires our emotional availability. What results is a sense of collaborating with God, a sense that God has stirred us and is making a connection with us. Likewise, Smith rejects the idea that inspiration comes from God as though from a long distance away: "The language of God up there inspiring me down here is alienating, part of a paradigm about God as a big person remote from me sending me messages," says Smith. Rather, God is indwelling, embodied in the preacher throughout this process. Referring to the hymn of St. Patrick's Breastplate, Smith speaks of the nuances involved in thinking of God as "before, behind, above, and beneath" us. This is a way of getting in touch with the very physical sensations we have of God's presence with us.

Smith's process of sermon preparation, especially in the phase of "hot thinking," is how the preacher himself is drawn into the experience of desire and ambivalence that always accompanies relationship with God, so that he can then invite hearers into this territory. When listening to a sermon, Smith tries to intuit whether the preacher has been in this place of conflict and dynamism. If so, then he feels he can trust and listen to her, but he is angered or bored by preachers who attempt to smooth over difficulties, or who appear to be engaging in a "calculated construction of a religious address," without venturing into the more dangerous territory of emotional openness, vulnerability to God, and conflict.

Crucial for reaching this state of emotional availability to God in which insights can occur is that a preacher engage with the diversity of human experience within himself. All preaching is preaching to oneself—anything a preacher says is directed at some aspect of herself; moreover, Smith believes that through a deep plumbing of one's own self, it is possible for preachers to connect with all aspects of human experience. Smith quotes Paul's claim to be "all things to all people . . . for the sake of the gospel" (1 Cor. 9:22–23). He also compares this aspect of the preaching vocation to acting, for an actor is someone who is in touch with the entire spectrum of humanity within herself, and this is how she is able to embody characters' experience without actually having those experiences herself. Likewise, by knowing himself fully, the preacher can understand the range of light and shadow in the human condition generally.

We [are] trapped . . . in many of our church services, and in our writing about faith, behind a screen of clichés. The connection between words and what they signify has been broken. The first human power—the power to name—is failing. For one reason or another, we choose not to break through. —*Nora Gallagher*

For preachers, this depth of understanding requires developing the capacity to reflect on their own religious experience. Smith advocate practices such as making retreats, sacramental confession, journal-writing, and undergoing spiritual direction. All of these practices help preachers to reflect on their spiritual lives; without such reflection, their preaching will be lacking. As an experienced spiritual director, Smith speaks of spiritual direction as an exacting practice in which preachers are held accountable for exploring their own experiences of desolation, consolation, attraction, and the various other affective states of our relationship to God. In spiritual direction people are asked to reflect on their availability or lack of availability to God, and discouraged from rationalizing and intellectualizing in order to stay close to the emotional drama of their own resistance or openness to

God. Most effective preachers have undergone this kind of coaching, which teaches them how to reflect on and articulate their experience with God. Smith cautions that unless preachers can engage their own religious experience in this way, they often feign it by becoming overly self-referential in sermons—telling anecdotes about themselves and so on. This kind of self-disclosure is actually a *substitute,* Smith warns, for genuinely self-revealing preaching that arises from deep engagement with one's own religious life.

If preachers are willing to go deeply into their own religious experience, they may well discover that God's good news comes to them precisely where they feel the greatest resistance to or distance from God. Powerful preaching often arises from this place of resistance to God. In fact, Smith suggests that it is the vocation of a preacher to tackle those difficult areas of life which, left to ourselves, we would avoid. God even saves certain people by making them preachers—this is the only way that they can wrestle with, come to understand, and finally move beyond their barriers to God. As preachers, says Smith, they get to feed from the same table at which they feed others, and he reminds us of the saying from Cardinal Mercier, "God calls you to be priests because he can no longer trust you as lay people." It is only by being priests and preachers that some people come to salvation.

Without preaching, Smith believes, the liturgy could become a self-contained repetition of traditional sayings about God, and even the Bible could be tamed. Our religious lives could become routine. Preaching breaks into these closed systems when the preacher dares to speak with passion about who God is and how God desires. Preaching is perhaps one of the only forms of discourse that can banish clichés about the divine, and really open us up to new experiences of God. The power of preaching to do this, while ultimately a mystery, has much to do with the preacher's own willingness to enter the messy and risky territory where God is at work in her own life. My sense of what makes Smith's preaching powerful and compelling is that it emerges from his willingness to enter this territory himself, as well as from his subtle and wise understanding of the geography and dynamics of the spiritual life. Over long years of ministry he has learned how to be in relationship to God and how to articulate this relationship; more than this, he has developed the spiritual courage to continue to encounter his own resistance to and longing for God, and speaks from this living experience with both authority and authenticity.

leadership in preaching

Mariann Edgar Budde is the rector of St. John the Baptist Episcopal Church, a congregation in Minneapolis, Minnesota, of about six hundred fifty members with an average Sunday attendance of three hundred. She has been the rector there since 1993, and so has learned how preaching can shape a congregation over time. Budde describes the role of preaching in the life of the church as the occasion when the preacher is able to expend time and effort to think deeply about a topic of significance and share these thoughts with the congregation. It is important that these ideas be grounded in Scripture in order to foster in the congregation a biblical imagination which can inform their lives and faith. Biblical images and stories are powerful, and Budde wants her hearers to be able to access that power through her sermons. As a preacher she spends time in this biblical world so that she can offer it to others, reminding them of this collective narrative of which we are a part.

Budde sees preaching as sacramental in a couple of ways. Through it people are consistently and dependably fed, as they are at the Eucharist. God is also present and active in preaching; there is a power in sermons that goes beyond anything the preacher herself can do—a sense of mystery, power, grace, and forgiveness. In addition, Budde feels strongly the presence of God when she is preparing sermons; in each and every sermon she preaches, God always provides something for her to say. She is constantly reminded of the miracle of the loaves and fishes: God always takes whatever she offers and makes of it something more than she could on her own. Finally, for Budde preaching is sacramental because in the context of eucharistic worship, it opens a space within its hearers to receive the sacrament. Thus the sermon and the sacrament are integrally connected.

Given her conviction that sermons can be an encounter with God, Budde thinks deeply about her own role in this event. She sees her task to be creating a moment and a space in which people can relax and listen; her responsibility is to trust that God is in that moment. It is also important that she not become too identified with her preaching, particularly because she is a good preacher, and expectations for her sermons are high. She does not worry about the outcome of the sermon, but only about offering it, recognizing that it is not about *her*, but about *God*. Furthermore, she knows that there can be times when she feels very in tune with the Spirit and yet is not, and times when she feels terrible about the sermon and yet the Spirit is working through it. Her feelings about the sermon can sometimes deceive her, and worrying too much about them would be another way of focusing more on herself while preaching than on God.

Like Martin Smith, Budde describes the relationship between herself and God in preaching by using the metaphor of acting, although her emphasis is somewhat different. She experiences the gap between her own sense of self and her role as preacher, the psychic distance between who she is in herself and who she is in that role. "I am putting all of myself into this role, but it is bigger than I am," she says. To put it slightly differently, "It is me doing this, but there is another me helping to make this happen." This is not the same thing as "faking it"; rather, she feels that what she embodies in this role is more than who she is on her own, even though she has to put all of herself into it. If the preacher is in some way a vehicle for God's revelation, then something more than herself is also present, working through her.

Projection is also a problem, Budde believes, for much is projected onto the preacher by the congregation, and to inhabit the role successfully means allowing others' projections to rest on the preacher lightly, without identifying with them. This projection is an inevitable part of the preacher's role in being "on display" and carrying out difficult spiritual work before a congregation, and, in a sense, on their behalf. For this reason, it is important that the preacher maintain a certain psychic distance from the role—a distance between the preacher and what the preacher is doing, even though it is the preacher who is doing it.

Budde sees her authority as a preacher as closely connected to her authority as rector and leader of her congregation. She has learned over time to claim this authority—to wear it lightly yet also not to minimize it. In preaching in particular she embodies the consistent voice of leadership that helps to hold a community together and shape it over time. While the community discerns collectively what their vision of the future might be, it is the rector who gives voice to the vision, particularly during preaching. If the rector does not carry out this task, then other members of the community will do it for him, just as one part of the body will compensate when another part of the body is not functioning correctly. Even though this articulation of vision is most visible in preaching, Budde emphasizes that it is only effective when the preacher's leadership is working well in other aspects of the community's life. The relationships between the rector and members of the community, the community's trust in the rector, the rector's ability to listen to and discern what is going on, a good sense of timing as to when and how to move the community forward, and the congregation's sense of the rector's integrity—all of these profoundly affect the preacher's authority and effectiveness. Budde feels that we have "too many prophets and not enough leaders in the Episcopal Church." By this she means that it is one thing to speak prophetically about individual and collective change, but quite another to provide leadership over the long haul in the painstaking work of change. Authoritative preaching occurs when it is part of this work of leadership.

For Budde, the authority of the preacher is intimately connected with her authenticity in the preaching role. In her book *Gathering Up the Fragments: Preaching as Spiritual Practice,* she points out that if preachers can experience preaching as a place to integrate the various dimensions of our lives, "where the important strands of my life in God and leadership come together," then this integration and the integrity that comes from it are an important source of the preacher's authority.[1] Budde mentions Parker Palmer's insight that we grant authority to people who lead undivided lives—in other words, people who have integrated both their inner and outer lives into one coherent whole.[2] Such people have integrity—their words, values, actions, and way of life hang together. This kind of authenticity and integrity on the part of the preacher is difficult to attain; seldom do our lives reflect the fullness of the gospel. There is thus a real danger of hypocrisy in preaching: Budde points to Jesus' injunction to the rich young ruler to give everything to the poor, which she has never done. Nevertheless, it is still possible to preach authentically on this text, provided she first feels the judgment of the text on her own life, then listens for how God might be moving her and the congregation forward to live more in alignment with this text. It is important that the preacher speaks the word of the text, even if she is not living it, if only so that this word can challenge her and the congregation to live this truth more deeply.

For Budde, authenticity in preaching is the sense that people hear her own voice when she is preaching, not someone else's, that she is fundamentally the same person in the pulpit as she is out of it. Like Smith, Budde notes that this authenticity is only gradually arrived at over time, in part because of the necessity of negotiating between a preacher's personhood and the role the preacher inhabits. It is also crucial that the preacher let the text speak to her first, before she offers it to others. "I am standing under the message," says Budde, "and assume it is for me, too." In this sense the text meets the preacher's personal experience, so personal history is part of the sermon.

Edwin Friedman's books on congregational leadership have been a major influence on Budde, especially his core insight that it is through gaining self-definition in the context of personal and familial relationships that leaders can function effectively amid the relational dynamics of congregations. Friedman states that "the self is an inexhaustible supply of sermons," which means in part that preaching is a primary way that the preacher discerns who she is in the midst of her personal and congregational relationships.[3] However, Budde is careful to qualify the ways in which personal experience is and is not useful in sermons. It is important that she speak from personal experience only so that others can benefit from it, and not in order to work out her own issues in front of the congregation. Discerning the difference between these two impulses emerges from the work of self-differentiation that Friedman advises for congregational leaders.

In keeping with these insights, Budde's practice of sermon preparation involves engaging Scripture and meditating on its meaning, as well as "listen[ing] to my life and the lives of those around me, holding the words of scripture as I pondered what, if anything, God might have to say."[4] This preparation process involves her body as well as her mind and spirit. She speaks of the importance of bringing body and mind into alignment, often at the beginning of the preparation process, through such activities as exercise, yoga, taking a walk, or even taking a nap. She knows that she needs to be grounded physically in order to think well, and to honor her body as part of the sermon process. She also realizes that she cannot take it for granted that body and mind are always in alignment, and that reaching this state takes work and awareness. Thinking about the preaching moment itself, she is aware of the importance of posture, tone, and physical presence, and she thinks about and works on these skills when preparing to preach. Once she is in the midst of the sermon, she does not think about these matters at all, which is in keeping with her belief that analyzing how she is doing while preaching is not productive.

The power of Mariann Budde's preaching, it seems to me, is grounded in the degree of integration that exists between her role as preacher, her role as rector and leader of a congregation, and her own personhood. Indeed, it is preaching that serves the function of integrating the various dimensions of her personal and vocational life. There is the sense that preaching emerges from and feeds back into both the life of the community she leads, and her personal life with God. Preaching then is not a task separated from the rest of her ministry, but is integral to its shape and expression. Her preaching also has power because it emerges from her keen understanding of her role as priest and leader, and her clarity about who she is in that role and how this relates to who she is personally. This clarity, developed over time, allows her to see how she needs to act in relation to the congregational system she leads; this clarity is expressed in her preaching through sermons that are fitting and helpful to those who hear. Clearly, too, the power of her preaching comes from her sense that God is at the center of preaching, and from the spiritual discipline she practices in order to allow space for God to speak in her sermons.

connecting scripture and our lives

Ellen F. Davis is unique among the preachers I interviewed for this book in that the primary exercise of her preaching ministry is not in the midst of a parish or mission congregation. Professor of Bible and Practical Theology at Duke Divinity School, she does the bulk of her preaching in an academic setting and sees it as intimately connected to her vocation of teaching. The goal of both her preaching and teaching is twofold: promoting intellectual understanding of the Bible and forming faith, by informing and transforming the imagination of the hearer. In her writings Davis notes that the English word "imagination" corresponds to the biblical word "heart," which is the organ of feeling and affection as well as thinking.[5] In preaching, therefore, to touch the imagination is to touch the heart, to touch the whole person. The goal of preaching is to help us imagine God more accurately, and thus to be moved toward repentance and transformation. Theological insight and personal transformation are also the goals in Davis's classroom teaching. The principal difference between teaching and preaching is in the rhetoric she uses, which is like the difference between prose and poetry. Whereas in lectures Davis will use discursive language, including a wealth of explanation and historical information, in preaching she will use poetic language that does not so much explain the text as "let it loose" to do its work of creating more profound theological insight and new moral vision in the church.[6]

Davis's preaching aims to instruct and transform the theological imagination, and thus her sermons are written in poetic, narrative, and image-rich language that speaks directly to the imagination. It is because of the rhetorical demands of preaching that she spends considerably more time on sermons than she does on lectures, since she labors over her choice of words in a disciplined use of language that parallels the practice of poets. Davis insists, however, that her teaching also aims to address and transform the theological imagination, in the sense that her teaching too is not just aimed at developing intellectual understanding of Scripture, but also a willingness to care about it and take its claims seriously.

Davis's sense of the similarity between preaching and teaching informs many of her beliefs about preaching and her way of approaching the task. Unlike some of the other preachers with whom I have spoken, Davis disputes the widespread Protestant claim that God is present and active in preaching in a particularly powerful way, akin to the way that God is present in the sacraments. Davis has a high doctrine of Scripture as the primary place where God speaks, and a high doctrine of the sacraments as a principal place where God is present, but not a high doctrine of preaching. Whereas the sacraments cannot fail, preaching certainly can, and Davis says she has "been let down too many times" to view preaching as an event in which God is particularly likely to be present. Furthermore, because as an Anglican she holds a high view of the sacraments, she does not need to locate God's presence in preaching.

This view of preaching may be one reason why Davis does not wrestle with questions about her authority as a preacher. She notes that authority is contextual and relational, and for this reason her preaching is probably most authoritative with her students, since they know her and respect her approach to and knowledge of Scripture, and thus come to her sermons with certain expectations that are likely to be met. By contrast, when preaching at church on Sunday morning, where the hearers do not know her or her approach to Scripture, and thus do not know what to expect from her, she feels she has no particular authority.

No preacher can ever be astonishing (in a positive sense!) unless she has first been astonished. And the only regular and fully reliable source of astonishment for the Christian preacher is Scripture itself.
—Ellen F. Davis

Davis's knowledge of Scripture, and even more her approach to reading it, are among the sources of the power of her preaching. She feels that preaching is meant to instruct the theological imagination to know God more fully, but often our imaginations are ill-equipped for the task either "because we are not really looking, or our vision is unfocused, or we don't know how to interpret what we are seeing, or, perhaps, because we are not spiritually well enough to see and understand."[7] Scripture can clear our clouded vision and disrupt our preconceptions, allowing us to see and imagine God more fully, but only if we read it in a certain way. Davis advocates a way of reading Scripture that she calls "ethical interpretation," which involves an attitude of curiosity, respect, and openness toward the unknown and the other. This attitude toward the text is the same as that which we would adopt in an ethical relationship to another person.[8] This is a stance that is open enough to allow for the possibility of being truly changed by the text. Humility, charity, and patience are the fundamental qualities of ethical interpretation. The stance of humility reminds us that none of our interpretations of the text are definitive, in part because of our sin-occluded vision. Charity involves a fundamental trust that the text, no matter how alien or even offensive it may seem to us, nonetheless has something to teach us. Patience involves dwelling with the text long enough to allow it to transform us.

Davis's practice of sermon preparation, evolving from these principles of ethical interpretation, involves "paying exquisite attention" to the text, reading it slowly and carefully enough, in its original language, for the text to be heard.[9] The preacher's position is as "first listener" to the Word; if she can hear it accurately, then she can convey what she believes both she and the congregation might need to hear in the text. Authenticity in preaching, Davis maintains, is this experience of hearing herself addressed by the Word; otherwise she will not be able to convey to her hearers how they might need to be addressed by Scripture. Davis departs from the Protestant claim that preaching is the Word of God, and holds a more nuanced view: the sermon can be called the Word of God only in that the sermon presents the experience of *receiving* the Word of God in Scripture. She emphasizes the role of the preacher as one who listens to and receives God's Word, more than as one who conveys or proclaims it.

As with poetry, the reader needs to bring intellect, emotion, and memory to her engagement with the Bible. This is also important since the text is addressing the imagination, not only the intellect, and thus calls the preacher to enter into the text in a personal way. As Davis reads and listens to Scripture, she will often jot down notes having to do with where the text intersects or speaks to her personal life. However, she almost never includes such personal examples in her sermons, nor does she appreciate them in the sermons she hears. She is critical of such personal stories because she feels they are often self-serving and self-indulgent, rather than being genuinely illuminating. Like Budde and Smith, then, Davis describes the meeting of the text and her personal experience as a necessary part of sermon preparation; it is crucial that the preacher wrestle with how this text informs her own life. All three preachers equally recognize the dangers of using this personal material overtly in sermons, although Davis is perhaps the most reluctant of the three to include it.

Davis is passionate about interpreting Scripture in response to the urgent public issues of the time, and this focus has only grown stronger in recent years. She is particularly concerned with the work of the church in the Sudan and with the ecological crisis, maintaining that the greatest challenge the church currently faces is to connect the moral vision engendered by Scripture to our material lives. As a scholar of the Old Testament, she feels that the Hebrew Scriptures in particular ought to be central to Christians' thinking and action on such matters, since these texts are so deeply concerned with our material, economic, and political lives. The Bible is less concerned with matters of personal salvation, she argues, than with the salvation that takes place in the social world. God demands that we "participate generously in God's work of bringing forth justice in history."[10] She dismisses as "unbiblical" the idea that preaching is supposed to be apolitical, concerned only with the private world of faith, and insists that if the church does not talk about social ills, such as the ecological crisis, it will lose credibility. Conversely, she finds that when she does mention these issues, those who listen tend to feel relieved that the truth has been spoken, rather than defensive. Davis is convinced that if preachers avoid dealing with these difficult public issues, it will threaten the validity of their entire ministry, as they are essentially refusing to participate in the most important work of the church today. By the same token, much of the validity, power, and authority of Davis's own preaching comes from her willingness to tackle these pressing issues.

The authenticity of Davis's preaching comes in part from her willingness to submit herself to the scriptural text, and to hear how it challenges her ordinary ways of thinking and living. How does her life match, or fail to match, what Scripture says and what she preaches? Here Davis prefers to speak of "integrity" rather than authenticity; she feels that the former points particularly to issues of character. Whereas authenticity suggests that one's words match one's inner self, integrity is about moral choices—how our words match what we do and how we live. For Davis, the personal integrity of the preacher means that the words he speaks and the life he lives are all of a piece. Thus Davis really does engage in the intense, focused, humble, and patient study of Scripture that she recommends to others. She also puts time and energy into the public issues on which she preaches, and strives to live in a sustainable way—walking instead of driving, using electricity sparingly.

Such questions of personal integrity are closely related to embodiment. Since she believes that Scripture ought to inform our material lives, Davis takes embodiment seriously: our interpretation of Scripture ought to inform our concrete decisions about what we eat, where we live, and how we live. Davis herself takes these choices very seriously, and this attention to her own material existence is an important part of the personal integrity that gives power to her preaching. The fact that she exercises and tends to her bodily health also gives her the energy she needs to preach and teach well, and in this way her relationship to her body is an important part of her preaching. Throughout Davis's writings, moreover, the preacher's relationship to Scripture is often described through metaphors of tasting, chewing, and swallowing. These metaphors point to Davis's own intimacy with the text, which she experiences physically as well as emotionally and spiritually. One way she experiences the text physically is by reading it aloud in Hebrew, so she and her students can savor the beauty of the language. Both preaching and teaching are powerful and draining physical experiences for her, and she often fasts before both.

In my conversations with Davis she did not seem to experience a tension between her inmost identity and who she is in her role as preacher. This may be in part because she sees preaching as so akin to teaching, and this is the role she also has outside the pulpit. It may also come from the fact that she is not ordained; perhaps it is the ordained who particularly feel that in preaching they take on a role with specific preconceptions and projections attached to it, as Budde describes. Finally, since Davis does not see the preaching event as one in which God is active in a particularly powerful way, Davis does not closely relate human speech and divine speech, and thus avoids the tensions and paradoxes that this relationship implies. Her role as preacher is to listen humbly, patiently, and charitably to Scripture, and this is what she is doing also when outside the pulpit—in her teaching, in her work in the public sphere, and in her personal life. Living on such intimate terms with Scripture, she is able to show how these texts can transform her hearers' imaginations, as they have transformed her own. What is most thrilling in Davis's preaching is her ability to show the astonishing and deeply true connections between Scripture and our lives.

Among the preachers I interviewed for this book, Jim Bradley holds the distinction of having preached for the longest place in one parish, as he has been the rector of St. John's Episcopal Parish in Waterbury, Connecticut, for over twenty years. St. John's is a downtown parish in an old New England industrial town, a formerly prosperous city that has suffered a decline in the past fifty years, as the industries there have largely folded. Fifty years ago there were quite a few vital Episcopal parishes in Waterbury; now St. John's alone remains. It is in large part due to Bradley's leadership that St. John's has flourished and grown in the last twenty years, and now also houses a thriving Hispanic congregation as well as ministering to the homeless population of Waterbury.

For Bradley, preaching is important in the life of a parish because preaching is the place where the story of the people is told. The story of the faith is the glue that holds the community together, and by "the story" Bradley means the story of Scripture, of the church in general, of the parish, and of the people, since all of these are in some sense one story. Without the telling and retelling of the story the church would suffer amnesia, not remembering who and whose we are. We get some of the story through hearing Scripture every Sunday, but preaching is the connective tissue that links these ancient texts with our lives today.

Preaching also describes and defines who we are as a people in relation to our story, but it should not proscribe or prescribe. Bradley admits that in his early years as a preacher he did sometimes preach prescriptive sermons full of shoulds and oughts, but he no longer does. In fact, he says that he quickly shuts down when someone starts telling him "the truth." Instead of using "you" in sermons, he now says "we"; the sermon is a conversation between himself and Scripture to which others are invited to listen. Thus he always begins his sermon preparation with the question, "What does this text say to me? How am I to understand this, or cope with this, or incorporate it into the conversation I am having with myself all the time?" Bradley does not believe that because he is a priest he has special insights that other people lack; his one advantage as a priest is that he is given the luxury of pondering these matters. Thus the key to reaching others in his sermons is to be honest with himself. If he is honest about his own response to the text, then he can have confidence that others may hear what he is saying as relevant for them too. In sermons he will often say, "I don't know about you, but I think...," which is a way of allowing listeners to form their own responses to what he says.

In addition to being in a conversation with Scripture, then, Bradley imagines himself to be in a conversation with his hearers when he is preaching. He is in a conversation with that part of his hearers that corresponds to the place in himself that the Scripture passage is addressing. There is no way of knowing this with complete certainty, but he feels he can often tell whether they share his experience and are touched by his words. What he is hoping to do in his preaching is to open a door in the hearers' minds and hearts, reaching both their intellects and their emotions. Since his preaching style is conversational and spontaneous, his sermons never feel like finished products, but instead are unfolding in the moment. He is comfortable adjusting his sermon on the spot if he feels that he has lost his hearers. This is something he teaches to the seminarian interns at St. John's, requiring them to preach without notes so that they can react and if necessary adjust to what is going on, experiencing the give-and-take of real communication. Bradley himself is a master at this: one time when I was there, a homeless and mentally ill person came into the church and walked down the aisle, ranting. Bradley stopped, listened to the man, welcomed him, invited him to sit down, and then continued his sermon. On another occasion, Bradley was talking about red-eye gravy when a member of the congregation interrupted him and asked how this gravy was made. Bradley stopped, gave the recipe, and then went on with the sermon.

In looking at the similarities between preaching and acting, Bradley argues that preaching is more like stand-up comedy than traditional theater, because stand-up comedy has the quality of spontaneous give-and-take that preachers need to develop. Comedians have to cultivate extraordinary responsiveness to their audiences and make immediate adjustments if they sense that they are losing their attention. As in stand-up comedy, sermons are like jokes; you either get them or you do not. There is a mysterious quality to a sermon, an element of the unexpected and inexplicable—if you have to explain it, it does not work, and the preacher does not get a second chance. And, like a funny event that cannot be recreated, you have to be there, which is one reason why sermons do not translate well to the written page. Although Bradley did not say this, I suspect that part of the intangible quality of a joke or a sermon has to do with the presence, timing, facial expressions, sense of ease, and temperament of the preacher—qualities that go far beyond the words that are spoken. Whether a sermon or a joke "works" also depends a great deal on the congregation, a phenomenon that Bradley notices when he preaches the same sermon at the 8 a.m. and 10 a.m. services on a given morning. A line that provoked a laugh at the first service will be greeted with stony silence at the next, for no obvious reason.

What makes preaching work, then, is a quality of extraordinary openness, awareness, and responsiveness to the present moment and what it requires. This openness depends in part on being able to enter into relationship with both the text and the hearers as though for the first time. Bradley explains this by drawing another parallel between preaching and acting. He notes that the task of actors is to make the familiar strange and then to make the strange familiar. Good actors rehearse a play rigorously and know it deeply; but when the curtain goes up, they need to act as though they have never said these lines before, and do not know what will happen next. In the case of really good actors, when the telephone rings onstage, they genuinely do not know who is on the other end of the line. The familiar has become foreign to them, in order for them to make it so for their audience as well. Likewise the preacher takes well-known texts from Scripture and makes them new for their hearers; and then, having done so, makes them familiar again.

I don't understand preaching, but I believe in it deeply.
— Ian Pitt-Watson

This atmosphere of spontaneity and informality is an aspect of Bradley's liturgical presence, and he finds this presence an important counterbalance to the formal structure and tone of the liturgy. The openness of his style allows for people to feel welcomed into the greater formality of the liturgy itself. He uses preaching particularly as an occasion for greater spontaneity within the service, so that the sermon creates a counterpoint to the more set nature of the liturgy. I find it interesting that Bradley goes to some lengths to cultivate this atmosphere of spontaneity. It does not just *happen,* but is created with care. This might seem to be a paradox, but the preacher has to train rigorously, as actors do, in order to create a feeling of freedom and informality that is not simply haphazard. "It takes a lot of work to be natural," says Bradley. For instance, a preacher has to practice for a long time before he can be comfortable enough to incorporate interruptions, like the recipe for red-eye gravy, and still continue. Bradley creates the experience of spontaneity so that the service can be more inviting, and yet he is doing this in a conscious and focused way. There is nothing sloppy, disorganized, or un-thought-through about this practice of informality.

Bradley's defense of "practiced spontaneity" seems to me to connect with the claims of both Budde and Smith that authenticity in the pulpit is not something that a beginning preacher steps into immediately; rather, it must be cultivated through a long apprenticeship, during which an exploration takes place of the relationship between the role of preacher and the selfhood of the one taking on this role. Only in this way can a preacher arrive at the ability to be completely present, conversational, and spontaneous in the preaching moment. Through taking on at a deep level the formal constraints of the preaching role in its liturgical context, and delving into the connections between this role and the self, one gradually comes to an ability to be authentically present in that role.

Bradley points out that authority, like authenticity, is never automatic; it has to be established relationally. Thus his authority as a preacher comes less from the official authority vested in him as a priest than from his connectedness to the congregation, and from the quality of his pastoral presence with them over time. His authority comes from his having shared the saddest and happiest times of his parishioners' lives with them; his presence with them at those times is what gives him authority in his preaching. Because what he says in his sermons coheres with who he is on an everyday basis with his congregation, his parishioners have adopted the attitude that whatever he says is important for them to hear. That is one critical source of both his authenticity and his authority.

For all his efforts to make the sermon spontaneous and informal, Bradley believes that preaching itself should never become a conversation. The basis of his authority, in his own eyes, comes at least in part from the fact that he has a theological education, and his hearers, for the most part, do not. So just as you would want an electrician rather than a plumber to fix an electrical problem in your house, so too it ought to be the theologically trained expert who preaches. For this reason, Bradley resists the recent phenomenon of making the sermon a conversation in which all members of the congregation may participate. If sermons become an opportunity for all to share their thoughts and feelings about a text, he believes, much of what makes the sermon valuable would be lost. Thus he upholds a fairly traditional view of the preacher's authority as well as a traditional image of the church as a valuable source of stability, continuity, and integrity. He feels that the church is countercultural in the kind of community it offers, and might be the last bastion of true community in this country, offering truer connection than Internet forms of social networking, for instance. Bradley also finds himself "fascinated and horrified" by the megachurch movement, which he believes to be creating communities governed by secular and consumerist norms, rather than a genuinely countercultural form of community. For example, he argues that megachurch liturgies are no longer "the people's work," but are entirely orchestrated by paid professionals whose chief goal is to entertain the congregants. In this sense, the life of these churches comes to mirror the kind of recreation found in secular culture, and not to provide something truly different.

The power of Bradley's preaching comes, it seems to me, in part from his poetic and evocative style. He opens avenues of vision but lets his hearers travel down them rather than holding their hands all the way. Even more than this, however, the power of his preaching comes from his unusual preaching *persona,* which mingles informality with a deep rootedness in tradition. He can seem almost like a clown or a fool sometimes, an iconoclastic figure who weakens people's defenses so they can hear a deeper truth. In taking on this unconventional expression of priestly and pastoral identity, he has found a way to be fully present as the person he is, while honoring the role he inhabits. In achieving this balance he is open to the mysterious power of the preaching moment, and invites hearers into this mystery as well.

telling the story

Zelda Kennedy is senior associate for pastoral care at All Saints Episcopal Church, a large parish of approximately four thousand parishioners and five full-time clergy in Pasadena, California, where she has served since 2003. Prior to that she was assistant rector at St. Patrick's Episcopal Church in Mooresville, North Carolina.

Kennedy is unique among those I interviewed for this book because although she is a compelling and powerful preacher, she insists that she does not like to preach and finds it an ongoing struggle. In part this is because of some negative public speaking experiences she had earlier in life that cause anxiety when she preaches. She has learned, therefore, that the best way to work with this anxiety is to shift her focus, placing less emphasis on herself and her performance and more on being God's instrument. This means that she always prays in private before preaching, asking that she will share God's Word in such a way that her congregation will be empowered to go out and be God's presence in the world during the week. Keeping the focus on God means "diminishing herself" when she is preaching, which works better at some times than others. On major feast days like Christmas and Easter, when she feels the pressure to "deliver something good," it is harder to let go of self-consciousness. At other times she is more able to step into the moment and allow the Spirit to transform her words.

When Kennedy's preaching is at its best, she likens it to moments playing basketball when she and the ball have become one. When this happens, she can be much more effective than when she is "forcing the play." For Kennedy, when self-consciousness and anxiety take over in preaching, this is akin to forcing the play. But when she and the sermon have become one, then a mysterious transformation takes place. She feels she is both there and not there, present while being absent. For her, this moment is when the experience of the sermon becomes sacramental, when God is using the preacher, just as God uses the elements of the Eucharist, to make God's presence known. She feels that she helps to provide this opportunity for her hearers to feel God's presence when she is able to be present with them herself. She particularly feels this when she preaches each week at the healing service, an intimate service in which she is able to connect with the congregation in a powerful way. She can look into their eyes and see whether what she is saying is relevant to them or not. When she senses a connection with the congregation, she feels that, through this connection, God becomes present to them also.

Preaching is also sacramental in that it offers something tangible to the hearers. Just as the sharing of the Body and Blood of Christ is an offering of something tangible, so too Kennedy wants her sermons to offer something concrete that people can take away with them, that becomes part of them, and that feeds them through the week. For this reason Kennedy gravitates toward storytelling in her preaching. Following Jesus, who used parables to explain the ethical and spiritual lessons he was teaching, Kennedy tells stories from everyday life so as to ground the truths of the gospel in human experience. She feels that it is a primary responsibility of preaching not only to explain the text, but to describe how it applies to our everyday lives, and she believes that stories do this most powerfully. Not only do they bring home the truth of the text, but they are solid enough for hearers to remember and hold on to. She recalls that when as a child she heard the words, "Once upon a time," she knew that she was about to hear something special; adults listen in a similar way to stories, believing that they will hear something magical and transforming.

The embrace of storytelling is one of the ways that Kennedy has brought her identity as an African-American woman into the pulpit. She notes that she never forgets that she is black and a woman; it is part of everything she does. Kennedy also believes that this is what others see when they first encounter her—first her race, then her gender—but she does not allow these stereotypical ways of seeing her to get in her way. She notes the importance of preaching with integrity, with the hope that eventually, in addition to noticing her race and gender, people will recognize her character—the fact that she is "an accomplished woman who has faced challenges and succeeded." To preach with integrity involves a combination of knowing who she is in the pulpit, in terms of her cultural particularity, and also allowing herself to be God's instrument, rather than keeping the focus on herself.

Preaching as an African-American woman to predominantly white congregations is inevitably an act of preaching across cultural difference. Being a storyteller is one way that Kennedy draws on black preaching traditions—using stories as way of highlighting the relevance of God's word to everyday life. She notices that a very different preaching style comes into play when she is preaching to a predominantly African-American congregation. The call-and-response exchange between preacher and hearers sets up a rhythm that she falls into naturally, and she finds the energy generated by this experience "amazing." However, she does not expect this kind of exchange to take place in white congregations, and she does not try to orchestrate it, even though occasionally, when she has succeeded in "stepping aside and letting the Spirit come through," she falls into a cadence that draws from black preaching traditions. In other words, she most fully taps into her cultural heritage when she is least self-conscious and most "at one with the game."

The stories Kennedy tells in the pulpit also draw from her identity as an African-American woman. For instance, she recently told a story about an incident of racial discrimination that she herself experienced while shopping, one that caused her hearers to feel outrage on her behalf, and led to some educational programming on racism at the parish. Kennedy also grew up knowing poverty at times, and she draws stories from this experience as well. She acknowledges the need for care and discernment in the use of this material; she feels uneasy when preachers tell personal stories as a way of processing their experience. The criteria she uses are these: Will this story be helpful to someone else? How would this story strike me if I were the listener? Can I tell the story without being emotionally overwhelmed by it?

Kennedy notes that preaching and celebrating the Eucharist at the weekly bilingual English/Spanish service at All Saints has greatly helped her to decide how and when to draw on her own culture and experience when preaching. Thinking about how the hearers' cultural background and experience shape their listening has made her more conscious of how she can use her own cultural identity most effectively. Preaching to this Latino community has also honed her abilities to offer something tangible in her preaching, since the lives of many of her hearers make it particularly important that preaching be relevant. Kennedy explains that because many of these congregants are wrestling with survival issues such as poverty or undocumented immigrant status, there is less room in sermons for abstract reflections, and a more pressing need to "get to the point," to present good news that can make a concrete difference in these circumstances.

The combination of Kennedy's high view of preaching as a place where God speaks and her own anxiety in preaching leads her to feel strongly that there is a difference between her preaching *persona* and her everyday self. "Zelda in the pulpit is about being God's presence in that moment," which means that she is definitely not the casual and relaxed person she is at other times. Partly because preaching as a manifestation of God's presence is an awesome responsibility, and partly because of the anxiety preaching causes, Kennedy says of her preaching experience: "In the pulpit I don't exhale; what I do is preach." At the door after church, she can be her usual relaxed self. She does not see the difference between pulpit *persona* and church-door *persona* as a problem, but rather as a gift, since it signals the exalted and important nature of the preaching event. Although preaching does draw a different *persona* from her than her ordinary self, she does not think of preaching as a performance, since this would suggest to her that the preacher had not done a good enough job stepping out of the way so that the Word could be heard.

The power of Kennedy's preaching comes from several sources. One source is simply the importance that she ascribes to preaching as an event in which God is present and speaking; another is the fact that she deliberately and prayerfully enters into both the preparation and the sermon event itself, asking that she become an instrument that God will use. Keeping the focus on God in her preaching rather than on herself to allay her anxiety has become a way to allow the Spirit in at a deep level. And then there is the power of her own life experience: her preaching reveals her comfort with her identity and her ability to make space for the identities of others. Kennedy is above all a consummate storyteller. She clearly thinks in stories, and thus is able to make convincing and memorable connections between the gospel and contemporary life. Kennedy's excellence as a preacher speaks to the importance for all preachers of being at home in their own skins, of knowing who they are and where they come from, in order to bring that knowledge into their preaching with clarity and wisdom, as she does.

the power of lay preaching

Stephanie Spellers is the priest and lead organizer of The Crossing, an emergent church community at St. Paul's Episcopal Cathedral in Boston, Massachusetts. She has served in this capacity since her ordination in 2005. Prior to that Spellers worked as a religion journalist and in higher education administration. Founded in April 2006, The Crossing is currently a community of some eighty members, with average weekly attendance of fifty people. It meets every Thursday at the cathedral for worship, Christian formation, and fellowship.

Preaching at The Crossing is unlike that in any other Episcopal church I have encountered because it is done principally by lay people, with guidance from Spellers and other leaders in the community. Preaching is one of the key places where the vision and calling of the community as the people of God is clarified and shaped, and many members of the community participate in this task. It evolved this way, Speller explains, because of the nature, genesis, and vision of this congregation. The congregation began with a process in which Spellers, after conducting numerous one-to-one relational meetings over a four-month period, gathered nine leaders interested in forming a new kind of church. These nine people met for five more months before the first public worship service, and it was this group together, not Spellers alone, who developed the vision for The Crossing. Because the birthing of the community was collaborative, born of a common vision, it made sense that the proclamation of this vision would also be shared by all. Furthermore, part of that vision is the celebration of "multivocality" rather than "univocality," which Spellers says is in keeping with the Anglican values of openness and comprehensiveness—the idea that no one person has a complete hold on the truth, and that many voices are needed to articulate it.

Despite this, The Crossing is not a leaderless community. The worship service includes an extemporaneous welcome, eucharistic prayer, and blessing, and those are the moments when Spellers proclaims and shapes the vision of the community. She also shares leadership in providing education and guidance to the lay preachers, who are identified and invited by the leaders of the community as well as Spellers herself and are given a structured format and process within which to develop their "reflections." The word "sermon" is not used, Spellers explains, because the word "sermon" can be too limiting; it often implies that someone is going to "talk at" the congregation, that the event will not be interactive, that the listeners are merely spectators and do not have to be involved. The Crossing tries to avoid loaded words or "church insider code"—hence the word "reflection" in place of "sermon" or "homily," since it is a word that people from outside the church can recognize.

The process of sermon preparation requires that the preacher study the Scriptures, which are always focused on the lectionary texts of the week, usually the gospel. For Spellers the focus on the lectionary is an essential dimension of teaching preachers that they preach as part of a larger tradition, reflecting on the same text that Christians all over the world are hearing on that Sunday. The use of the lectionary is one way that The Crossing stays connected to the Episcopal Church and the larger Christian faith. The preacher studies the Scripture texts always with at least one other member of The Crossing community, thus emphasizing the idea that the community breaks open the Word together. Spellers notes that preachers are not required to do extensive exegetical research, but they know where those resources can be found.

Preachers at The Crossing are required, however, to connect the Scripture texts explicitly with their own personal story, showing how the passage matters to them. When preachers reveal where they struggle with the text and with God, other members of the community can see where they can connect to the text, and can feel that they are all in this search together. The telling of personal stories is what makes community happen. The value placed on personal stories is so high, Spellers says, that without them there is a sense that the preacher skimmed the surface but did not go "all the way in." This emphasis on the personal, moreover, is connected to the ecclesiology of The Crossing, which Spellers calls a "discipling environment." The church is not only the place where people gather to praise God and be refueled for their lives, but also where they *practice* becoming messengers of the reign of God, which is their task during the rest of their week. Through preaching, members of the community learn how to connect their stories to God's story, and then they can proclaim this connection in their lives outside the church. In this way, the church is like a school for evangelists.

In addition to connecting with their personal stories, preachers at The Crossing must also explicitly connect the text with the common story of the other members of the church and of the world outside. In this way, preaching is not simply personal testimony, but expands to communal and political dimensions. Finally, the sermon must include some kind of charge to the congregation, something the members need to do in relation to what has been proclaimed.

Once the sermon has been written, it is sent to Spellers and another Crossing leader for feedback, which is incorporated into the final draft. At this stage Spellers educates and coaches preachers; she sees herself as teaching them how to read the text of Scripture, the text of their own lives, and the text of the world. After the reflection is preached in the worship service, members of the congregation are able to offer their own reflections in response; usually four to five people speak for a minute or less. These responses are part of the preaching event, and preachers are routinely surprised at how deeply the community listens and carries forward their own reflection. Thus preaching at The Crossing is a communal practice from beginning to end: no preacher develops his or her sermon in isolation, and the preaching event itself is "owned" by the whole community.

The practice of preaching at The Crossing also shows, in microcosm, how Spellers views her own leadership role in the community. Rather than ceding her authority, she uses it to facilitate the leadership of others. The leadership model she relies on is that of community organizer, which is part of her own background. The task of the community organizer is to "be constantly listening for people's gifts, noticing where they need to grow, helping them to discover voice, claim power, learn how to exercise power, all for the sake of a common purpose, God's purpose." This kind of leadership fits perfectly with Spellers's ordination vows, in which she promised to facilitate the ministries of all believers. The assistance and training that Spellers provides to preachers in the community is one example of this, and she describes the amazing transformation in the lives of those laity who discover that they have a powerful voice with which to preach the gospel.

Seeing these transformations, Spellers is baffled as to why other churches do not adopt lay preaching. "We complain that the laity don't know how to do evangelism, but maybe this is because the priest won't be quiet and let the people do the proclamation, and learn how to become messengers of the reign of God." Commenting on the lack of lay preaching in the Episcopal Church, Spellers also notes the resistance that she has encountered from other clergy to lay preaching at The Crossing. This resistance shows her that preaching is the last bastion of clerical privilege, making her even more convinced of the necessity of lay preaching.

Recently Spellers has begun to preach at the first worship service of the month. The request that she preach more frequently arose not because people were dissatisfied with lay preachers, but because the community realized there is something unique about Spellers's role—about the way she, as priest, holds the community and its vision. Using L. William Countryman's description of the priest as the one who lives "on the border of the holy" so as to invite others to journey there,[11] Spellers feels that as the one who most intentionally lives on that border, she does have a unique perspective on the life of the community that others want to hear, even though the lay voice is still primary.

Spellers describes authenticity in preaching as the experience of the Word coming from the core of who she is and who God created her to be; paradoxically, she notes, it is when God inhabits us that we become truly the selves we are meant to be. Interestingly, Spellers finds it more of a challenge to find this authentic voice in preaching than in other parts of the service, such as the welcome, the eucharistic prayer, and the blessing. Perhaps because Spellers delivers these parts of the service extemporaneously, she finds herself listening more deeply both to the community and to God. She has a feeling of throwing herself open to God as if to ask, "Can we do something here together? Would you use me to say the Word that needs to be spoken in this prayer?" This gives her a powerful sense of being a channel, of speaking truths so deep she did not know them until she spoke them, being truly herself and at the same time "completely synched up with God." When "the door opens" in her she is able to sense what is going on in the community, and also to articulate it.

There are clearly some major advantages in the approach to preaching practiced at The Crossing. For one thing, this practice alleviates some of the difficulties with preaching that I described in chapter 1—namely, the way in which the preacher is the only person whose faith and life are on the line, whereas the listeners are spectators who have no ownership of the event. At The Crossing, by contrast, preaching is owned by the community as a whole, and thus there is a greater sense of involvement on the part of both preacher and listeners. For this reason it becomes easier to find authenticity in preaching, and to exercise authority in a way that uses power on behalf of the community, and thus is not prone to the danger of authoritarianism implicit in traditional preaching practices.

Perhaps the biggest criticism that could be leveled against this preaching practice, and one that Spellers has heard often, is that it does not carry forward the Scripture and tradition of the church powerfully enough, given the widespread biblical illiteracy of our times. Spellers responds by noting the various ways that the preaching of The Crossing stays true to Anglican tradition, with its insistence on the centrality of Scripture. She insists that all preaching at The Crossing stay focused on Scripture: "This is the Word of God; it has traveled to us, come among us.... I trust that God is breaking something open in our lives using that Word." She also points out that the emphasis on the intersection of the Word of God and the preacher's life is in keeping with the threefold source of authority in Anglicanism—Scripture, reason, and tradition—while its focus on spiritual practices connects with the Incarnation as a central doctrine of Christian faith. Far from allowing the richness of Scripture and tradition to be lost, through lay preaching all members of the community grapple with Scripture and tradition more deeply, and come to understand it better. For many churches Scripture and tradition are the exoskeleton, the forms that define the community on the outside, but at The Crossing Scripture and tradition are the endoskeleton, powerfully defining it in ways less easily seen from the outside.

resonance in preaching

Michael Curry, who has been bishop of the Diocese of North Carolina since 2000, is considered one of the best preachers in the Episcopal Church. Prior to his episcopal ordination, Curry served churches in Baltimore, Maryland; Lincoln Heights, Ohio; and Winston-Salem, North Carolina.

According to Curry, people come to church with a deep hunger, and the liturgy feeds this hunger in various ways—the Eucharist feeds our longings in more subtle ways, the sermon more directly and explicitly. Preaching names both our struggles and our hopes; it does not tell us things we do not already know, but it brings them to our conscious attention, and this naming itself makes the chaos of life more manageable. The profound disappointment we feel when preaching does not feed our longing stems from our hope that it will indeed "lift a Word that engages that hunger."

Curry insists that the naming of hope that preaching provides ought to take the form of *proclaiming* rather than *explaining* this hope. To this end, Curry relies greatly on storytelling in his sermons, both retelling the story of the reading for the day and telling stories from our lives that connect with the text. He points out that stories ought to tell themselves; if you have to explain them, then you have not told the story the right way. The mysteries of the faith cannot be explained, but only confessed. The explanatory mode is the one that seeks to dissect these mysteries and make sense of them, whereas in Curry's view they are meant to be proclaimed. The church's creeds, for instance, were meant to be sung rather than recited; they are doxology, and thus cannot be analyzed or explained. Similarly, preaching is not meant to explain and make sense of the claims of the faith, but to sing them. Curry notes that if in preparing his sermons he finds himself explaining something, he takes it as a sign that he does not yet fully understand what he is talking about—it is not yet "in his gut."

In part because of the deep hunger that people feel for a word of hope, Curry feels that preachers have more authority than they usually realize, even with younger people who are more suspicious of authority. People grant a preacher authority in part because he or she is a "publicly spiritual person" whose life is given over to the service of God, a person who has prepared and studied and who has been commissioned for this work by the church. People look to such individuals for guidance. Curry acknowledges, however, that a preacher can squander that authority pretty quickly, and so what is also needed is a less institutional and more personal kind of authority based on living with authenticity and integrity. Even though the relationship between what we preach and how we live is "dialectical," there needs to be a perceptible relationship between the two. A sense of congruence between the message preached and the life lived is what conveys authority.

Finally, the message preached has its own authority if the preacher has prepared in a certain way. Curry explains this using the image of resonance, which he has learned about through his studies of the violin. "Resonance is the key to beauty in playing the violin," says Curry. If a violin player plays a D on the G string, and hits it just right, then the D string will vibrate, and this adds immeasurably to the beauty of the sound. Applying this practice as a metaphor for preaching, Curry says that "when the message hits, when I am hitting the D on the G string, and your D string starts singing, that has its own authority.... Then something else is going on that's beyond all of us. That's when the Word becomes flesh and dwells among us."

As this description suggests, Curry is convinced that God is active in the preaching event even though it is hard to say how. Although God's presence can at times be felt, he warns that traditional outward signs of the presence of the Spirit may be misleading. For instance, in the African-American Baptist tradition of Curry's childhood, the presence of "the shout" was supposedly a sign of the Spirit's movement. However, since members of the congregation often knew in advance who was going to shout and when, this dramatic expression was not always an accurate sign. It is necessary to "test the spirits" and discern what is really happening.

Can the preacher actually facilitate God becoming present? On the one hand, Curry notes that God's "showing up" in the sermon or liturgy is unpredictable and may not have to do with the preacher. On the other hand, as his violin metaphor suggests, there are things the preacher can do to help create the experience of resonance—that moment when what the preacher says touches something in the hearer, and when something beyond the human breaks into the moment. For one thing, creating resonance requires discipline and practice in preaching, just as it does in playing the violin. It also requires the spiritual discipline of the preacher opening himself to God, and this has to happen in the preparation process as well as in the moment of preaching.

The goal of Curry's preparation process, therefore, is to get to the point where the sermon is speaking to him; when his own string is vibrating, then he knows that someone else's might vibrate as well. The sermon needs to speak to all of him—heart, soul, mind, and gut—since God touches all of these parts of our being, just as a good meal touches all of the senses. If a sermon is only a head trip, or only plays on the emotions, then it is not ready, not fully "cooked." There is no formula for getting to this point except to continue living with the sermon, cogitating over it, praying over it. As an extrovert, Curry finds that he often speaks his sermons aloud, and walks around the room while doing so, engaging his body and voice to help create the moment when the sermon speaks to him. Although in this process he asks where the sermon speaks to him personally, he is very careful in how he refers to himself in sermons, so that the sermon does not become too focused on him.

Once Curry knows how the sermon speaks to him, and how he responds to it, then his next challenge is to get this message across. Here Curry relies on his experience and his gift for preaching to many different kinds of people. Curry developed this ability out of necessity; as an African-American he grew up learning how to communicate in multiple worlds. As Curry points out, any group that is not the dominant culture has to be bilingual and biracial, knowing their own language and that of the culture that surrounds them. This experience has helped Curry to develop the intuitive grasp of how to cross cultural boundaries that is such a strong mark of his preaching. In addition, the predominantly African-American congregations that he served before becoming bishop were socially and economically diverse, so he was preaching to multiple populations within the same congregation.

Curry's practices of storytelling and of proclaiming rather than explaining were effective in reaching such diverse groups. Another helpful strategy was focusing on one strong point to the sermon, a take-away message that people would be thinking about all week. To reinforce this, he always chose a title for his sermons, printed this in the bulletin, and often asked members of the congregation to repeat it both to him and to each other. This focus on one message allowed him to "deal with what was truly simple and therefore deeply complex," rather than making so many smaller points that no one knew what he was talking about. Clarity became especially important when he was preaching to a diverse congregation.

Curry's own style of preaching incorporates the inflections, cadence, and rhythms of the black Baptist preaching he heard growing up, and uses call-and-response and a wide range of emotional expression. In some of the African-American congregations he served before becoming bishop, especially those that were used to the sermon as "the presentation of a learned discourse," his preaching style was "a bit of a jolt." Some parishioners left his churches; "for them, anything that smacks of too much ethnicity is calling them back to a place they don't want to go to." As bishop, his challenge is preaching to predominantly white congregations, who may not be used to his preaching style or as fully able to participate in it. At the outset of Curry's episcopate, members of the diocese made certain assumptions based on his preaching style—either that he was a conservative evangelical or that, as a black man, he subscribed fully to a liberal agenda. And sometimes children say, "Is he mad at us? Why is he shouting?" because they are not used to the emotion and passion of his preaching. Curry also acknowledges that he can be more at ease in preaching to African-American congregations because they share a common history and culture, so that he can draw on shared metaphors and be readily understood.

On the whole, however, Curry has not found it terribly difficult to bridge the cultural differences between his preaching style and white congregations. He believes that the relative ease with which he has done this stems from the fact that the hunger that all people feel for a word of hope is so deep that they will readily adjust to any style of preaching if they find that the message touches them. In addition, however, Curry consciously strives to begin each sermon with an introduction that establishes common ground between himself and the congregation before launching into the sermon itself. Often these introductions initiate a conversation with the congregation; for instance, he may say something that provokes a laugh, or may ask them a question, or ask them to say something to their neighbor in the pew. Occasionally he will engage white congregations in call-and-response, often in a light-hearted way—"Someone has to give me an Amen here, just help me out a bit!" Often the congregation will laugh and then do what he asks. Curry also notes that the rhythm of call-and-response may very well be happening between himself and the congregation even when they are silent; as he watches their bodies, he can tell if they are "rocking with his rhythm." He can tell if they are "shouting with him," even if they make no sound. He is able to tell whether or not a dialogue is taking place. So important is conversation with a congregation to Curry's preaching that once, when he preached for a radio broadcast, without anyone else present, he felt that he was not preaching at all.

Curry argues that there is a strong theological rationale for preaching conversationally. Even though the authority of the preacher is real, it cannot be a word spoken "from on high." If preaching becomes overly hierarchical, it is too much about the preacher, and not enough about preacher and congregation together welcoming a transcendent word. He likens preaching to the conversation between the two disciples on the road to Emmaus, when they were talking over their experience with God, and then, inexplicably, God in Christ himself showed up and walked with them.

Preaching as a bishop, which Curry describes as being like "a traveling evangelist, or a circuit rider," poses its own particular challenges. One challenge of preaching to many different congregations is that he does not have "automatic conversational space" with the congregation, as a parish priest would have, and so this space and these relationships have to be reestablished each time. Furthermore, given the demands of the job and the frequency of his preaching, he cannot prepare a new sermon each time he preaches. Instead, he prepares one sermon for each liturgical season that captures the major themes of the season, and then this core message evolves with each sermon.

As a celebrated preacher, Curry has had to wrestle with not making his own excellence an idol. He has to remind himself at times that he does not have to be great, he just has to preach. He periodically reminds himself that he is preaching the Lord and not himself, that he needs to "get off the pedestal, and get back where you are supposed to be." Surely Curry's focus on God, rather than on his own prowess, is part of what makes him an excellent preacher. His own personal wrestling with the sermon until he reaches the point where it speaks to him also allows him to speak from a deep place to others. In addition to this interior work, Curry also has a superb intuitive sense of how to connect with people. This serves him well both as bishop, where he has to work to reestablish these connections each time he preaches, and also as an African-American preaching to predominantly white congregations, where he has to work to establish common ground across cultural difference. This ability allows him to tap the richness of the black preaching tradition in ways that connect authentically even with those who do not share that tradition. All of these skills and spiritual disciplines together enable Curry to create a deep sense of resonance when he preaches, and thus to facilitate the experience that something greater than the human has become flesh among us.

transforming encounter with God

When Susan Burns arrived at Church of the Redeemer in Bethesda, Maryland, in 1994, the church had been in crisis and had lost many of its members. She resolved not to try to "fix" the parish, but rather "to stand up every Sunday and preach the gospel as best I understand it at this time and in this place." Over the years the church has turned around completely, becoming a vibrant and growing congregation. Burns's preaching has had a great deal to do with this transformation, as it has been central to her leadership from the beginning, and many members say that what drew them to the parish was the excellent preaching.

For Burns, the essential role of preaching in the church is to be a place where the community hears from someone who has been set aside to study the Scripture texts, to "consider" them, in the literal sense of "sitting-with" them. Unless someone has taken this time with the text, the Word will be only words and will not engage the hearers. On the other hand, to hear from a preacher who is "filled up with the Word" excites people and helps them to encounter God's Word in their own lives. Her hope is that in the sermon moment people will feel not just that they are hearing a report about what God did at one time in the past, but experience God's action at that very moment. She wants to draw hearers into the challenge of the text and show them that the Spirit is present in this word. She wants them to experience the deepest reality in which we live—not merely the reality of the world around us, but the reality that the kingdom of God is happening among us now as it was back then. Burns hesitates to say that God is speaking through her preaching, but she does feel that she is in a conversation with God as well as with the congregation. As a result people are energized by her preaching because they come to it with the expectation that they will meet God there.

In order to convey the sense that the sermon is an event of God's presence, Burns cultivates that relationship with God in her preparation process, which is one of wrestling with God and with the text. After she completes her exegetical work on the Scripture passages, the moment arrives when she has to "go to the mat" and decide what she believes the text is saying. She experiences God as "egging her on" in these moments, saying, in effect, "I have given you this great material. Now show me what you've got." For Burns, authenticity in preaching emerges from the sense that she has thrown herself fully into this relationship with the text, and has come to the point where she knows what this Scripture means to her today, how it connects with her own life and that of the congregation. It is important that the sermon emerge from her own sense of what the Scriptures are saying and not be someone else's ideas, and she also tries to leave her own agenda to one side. There is a paradox at work here: the sermon is not about herself, and yet it is deeply personal because she is fully implicated in it. A preacher needs to be present in her sermon; as Burns says, "If you are trying to hide, people see that anyway. Don't think they don't see it. They may not be verbalizing it, or thinking it consciously, but they know, and when they see that, then they won't trust you." It is important that the preacher not lie, that she say only what she knows to be true and avoid pretending to be wiser than she actually is. It is also important that the preacher not strive to preach the "right" sermon on the text, but rather the one that is in her at the particular time and place in which she is preaching.

For Burns, an authentic encounter with God, text, and congregation is one important basis for her authority as a preacher. Her authority comes from the fact that she is in a living relationship with God, which is expressed in her preaching. In her role as preacher she is both the same as those to whom she speaks, and also different. Since she is representing God and the church, she has certain responsibilities in how she speaks and what she says. While her preaching is conversational, she must speak with a certain amount of decorum because of her representative role. Above all, however, she needs to maintain her integrity— to be honest and to be herself—because this is the best way to represent God. Like every preacher, Burns must constantly negotiate the relationship between who she is in herself, and who she is in her role as a preacher; her authority and authenticity come from doing this adeptly.

Another important source of her authority is the way in which she fulfills her pastorate outside the pulpit. When people know that she cares about them, that she follows through with her responsibilities as rector, that she lives a life of integrity in general, then they will grant her greater authority in her preaching. True authority in preaching, then, has everything to do with the person she is in all aspects of her life, and the trust that her congregation has learned to place in her.

Burns finds that one way to engage deeply with the text is to learn it by heart and perform it before preaching the sermon. Part of the power of this performance practice is that it consciously engages the body in the preaching event. Burns notes that learning these practices has made her more conscious in general that when she is preaching, she is communicating with her body as well as with her voice. She thinks through what kinds of gestures she might use to make her message more vivid and is very aware of how she is standing—if she is up on her tiptoes, for instance, or standing on one foot. Over all, what her body communicates in the sermon is a sense of energy, a sense of "I'm coming at you. I've got something to say here." Her manner, body, and voice all convey a sense of excitement and playful delight. Her body is fully engaged throughout the liturgy, so much so that at times she says she has difficulty restraining herself from inviting everyone in the congregation to dance.

One of the sources of Burns's effectiveness as a preacher is the collaborative nature of her preaching practice. She and the other clergy in her parish regularly share sermon drafts with each other, and give each other feedback on these drafts. In addition, the parish holds a midweek Eucharist, in which the readings of the following Sunday are used, and those present reflect on the texts together. At monthly vestry meetings the same practice is used. This means that on most weeks Burns has discussed the Scripture texts with members of the congregation beforehand, and incorporates their questions and insights into the sermon. This input makes the sermon conversational in two important ways: it explicitly draws on the lives and thoughts of members of the congregation, and it is preached in the presence of those who are particularly interested in hearing how Burns develops their ideas into the sermon. Thus in the preaching there is a sense of a real conversation, of energy coming back from the hearers instead of the communication only going one way. This adds to Burns's sense of energy and playfulness in the preaching moment.

The power of Burns's preaching stems from her deep conviction that preaching is central to her ministry and to the life of the church. This conviction gives her the courage to move through the inevitable fear of preaching, and to enter deeply into relationship with God and God's Word in the preaching process. Engaging the Word with her body as well as her mind and spirit is a vital part of cultivating this deep and transforming relationship. Inclusion of the congregation in this process is also vital to the insight and energy generated by it. The result of this process is the enthusiasm and delight that are evident in her preaching, and in those who are listening. In hearing Burns preach, listeners have a sense that something is really happening, that God is really going to show up. Burns is a preacher who believes strongly in the transformative power of preaching, and has demonstrated in her own parish the veracity of this belief.

chapter four

Engaging the Body in Preaching

And here we offer and present unto thee, O Lord, our selves, our souls and bodies, to be a reasonable, holy, and living sacrifice unto thee. — Rite I, Eucharistic Prayer 1,
The Book of Common Prayer 1979

In the previous chapter we heard from preachers who strive to achieve both authenticity and authority in the pulpit through careful preparation and the development of personal presence, rooted in the body. We found that what unites these preachers is a deep personal engagement with Scripture, God, congregation, and self in their approach to preaching. All eight have also meditated on the relationship between their "everyday" selves and their role as worship leaders, between private personhood and public *persona*. And all of them have found ways to engage fully and holistically with the preaching task, bringing their bodies as well as their minds and spirits to preaching.

While each person's preaching style is different, all preachers can benefit from the use of concrete tools and practices that lead to an increased sense of engagement, authenticity, and authority. A wealth of practices is available to help with this, ranging from private prayer to exercises that engage the imagination to group discussion of the texts. For some of the preachers I interviewed, the use of the body is central to their preaching. In this chapter, we will focus on four such practices:

* a method of freeing the voice for proclamation;

* yoga and movement practices that free the body for fuller expressiveness;

* the performance of Scripture texts; and

* practices of improvisation.

Involving the body in specific practices such as these is a concrete way of bringing the whole self more fully to the preaching moment, finding the presence of God in the preaching moment, feeling the truth of the text in our bodies and voices, and connecting to the congregation. Integrating our bodies into the preaching moment allows us physically to feel an authentic way to inhabit the relationships that make up preaching—with self, God, hearers, and text. The presence that we learn through these physical practices will not take away the fear of preaching, but they will teach us how to be present through the fear.

freeing the voice for proclamation

If preaching is going to be an incarnational event, the Word of God becoming flesh and dwelling among us, then this requires of preachers a willingness to bring *all* of themselves to the preaching moment, and to be present in body, mind, and spirit. Certain methods of physical and vocal training can teach us how to be more fully present in our speaking, involving the body as well as the mind and spirit in the work of proclamation. One approach to training the voice and body for such embodied communication is found in the work of Kristin Linklater, a teacher of voice for actors. She argues that each person is born with a voice capable of expressing, through a two-to-four-octave pitch range, the fullness of his or her thought and feeling.[1] Social conditioning, trauma, and the tensions of daily life, however, often diminish and distort this expressiveness. The voice becomes disconnected from the body, unsupported by the breath, and is squeezed out by overworking the throat, jaw, and tongue muscles. Such speaking leads to the divorce of words from meaning and emotion, such that words *describe* rather than *reveal* the content of which they speak. The speaker whose voice is thus distorted no longer fully inhabits her words; although she may be speaking to others, she is not fully present in her words. Instead of being connected to what she is saying, she is talking *about* it, from a safe distance—"phoning it in," as actors put it.

The process of teaching students how to be present in their speaking involves helping them reconnect their voices to their bodies and emotions. Linklater's method of voice training takes students through a series of exercises that teach physical alignment, diaphragmatic breathing, relaxation of throat muscles, connecting voice with breath, and the use of the body's natural resonators to amplify the voice. As actors practice these exercises, they gain an increased sense of presence and truthfulness in their speaking. This approach to vocal training offers insight into what fully embodied communication is, and how it is experienced in the body. Fully embodied communication depends on the freedom of the voice in the body, the connection of the voice to breath and emotion. When we speak with this freedom and connection, we are not just speaking words, but we are claiming the words fully; the words are living in our bodies. We are able to say what we mean and mean what we say. The meaning of the words is communicated in the words we speak. Our whole selves are communicating the words, which is another way of saying that we are fully present in this act of communication. To be able to communicate in this way is a matter of spiritual and psychological growth, but it is also a matter of physical and vocal training, learning methods of relaxation, alignment, and breathing that allow for the freedom of the voice.

Conversely, this approach to voice training indicates what gets in the way of our embodying a sermon fully, such as tension in the belly that prevents breath from fully expanding the lungs, and tension in the throat that closes off the sound. These physical blocks to the free voice point to spiritual and psychological blocks, ways of thinking and beliefs about ourselves that prevent us from fully claiming our words, being able to say what we mean and mean what we say. We can work on these blocks at a spiritual and emotional level, but we can also work on them physically, for instance by learning how to relax the belly muscles so that the breath can freely enter and leave our bodies, and relaxing the throat muscles so that the voice can express itself unimpeded. We can learn how to be more fully expressive through certain physical practices— of alignment, breathing, natural use of the voice.

Through learning these skills our bodies actually teach our minds and spirits how to be present; we discover in our bodies what it feels like to be fully present. As we engage these practices, our bodies can also teach us what we need to say in our preaching. Perhaps at times we are unsure of what we need to say, or we have repressed deeper and more dangerous truths than the ones we habitually express. However, our bodies house these truths, and when we begin to connect our words with our breath living in the body, these truths may rise to the surface and demand to be expressed. In this sense the Linklater work is a form of spiritual direction—it helps preachers delve deeper into themselves to discover what they truly believe. As Martin Smith notes, what makes preaching alive is the sense that the preacher is honestly wrestling with what is really going on between himself and God. This wrestling can be done on a purely spiritual level, but the Linklater voice work offers a way of allowing the body to provide insight into what is going on spiritually.

> The way forward for me lay in using a different part of myself to judge between true and false. The best way I can describe it is moving down from my head into my stomach. . . . The stomach doesn't work visually but viscerally. It "sees" in the dark, but if listened to carefully, gives reliable guidance. It ties itself in knots when you're lying, and tells you what to do even before you have worked out why that should be right. . . . The head tells you what could be, the stomach tells you what is.
> —*Gwyneth Lewis*

I have often seen my students happen upon these insights as they practice this voice method, and begin to allow their bodies to tell them what they need to say. For instance, one student came to class feeling confused about what she wanted to say in the sermon she was preparing. Once she began connecting her breath to her voice and inhabiting her words more fully, however, she discovered the risky yet necessary words she needed to speak, hidden from her conscious mind but lodged in her body. Another student could not forge an authentic connection between her breath, her voice, and the words on the page that she had written. It was only when she finally made this connection that it became clear to her that the sermon she had written was not what she really wanted to say; her mind did not know this, but her body did. A third student found that when he tried to connect the words he had written to his true feelings about the biblical scene he was describing—Jesus returning from the grave and speaking to his disciples—he discovered a completely different emotional tone to his words, which also changed the words themselves. A fourth student had written a sermon that castigated people for their lack of faith, which was actually what she was feeling about herself. Once she connected more deeply to the words, she found a new level of compassion for the doubts that she was describing (in herself and others), and also a new level of certainty and authority in her proclamation of faith underneath those doubts. In each case, what allowed for authentic preaching was the acceptance of some part of the self that had previously been rejected, and this integration came about through physical practices.

Such training also assists preachers in becoming more confident in their physical presence when preaching, and thus offers a way of working on common problems. *What do I do with my hands while preaching? Should I use gestures? What is my body language saying? How do I project my voice?* Too often we try to solve these problems superficially— for instance, a preacher will note in his manuscript where he wants to make a gesture. Or he will become aware of a mannerism or tic, such as a habitual hand gesture, and try to control it during the sermon. Or he will respond to complaints that he cannot be heard by shouting. These "solutions" work from the outside in, and as a result they promote self-consciousness, the mortal enemy of preaching. The Linklater voice training approach, by contrast, works from the inside out. When the preacher finds an organic, internal connection between the words he is saying and the emotions and meaning contained in the words, then these questions about gestures and body language take care of themselves. Such training is "transformative" in the deepest sense, in that it changes the form, the shape, of the person doing it, and does so from the inside.

This voice work is fundamentally based on the freedom of the breath. The free voice depends on breath easily entering and leaving the body, with enough breath to sustain the thought and feeling expressed in the voice. As we observed in chapter 2, one of the best and closest experiences of God's relationship to us is the physical experience of breath in the body, because the breath is something beyond our control yet also something that we need to allow to happen. Breath is infinite, yet intimate and necessary to our very life. It is no accident that the Holy Spirit, that aspect of God who brings God into our very being, is known in Hebrew as *ruach* and in Greek as *pneuma,* both of which can mean breath. To feel the breath in the body is to feel the Spirit's presence within us, and the voice work teaches us how to allow this free breath to enter and leave us. In a very concrete way it teaches how to allow God to be truly with us, breathing in us, while remaining ourselves. In this sense, the free breath is an experience of how to negotiate the paradoxical relationship with God that is at the heart of preaching.

At the deepest and simplest level, this voice work is about teaching people how to be present with God, self, and hearers in their speaking. As a way of teaching this experience, I do the following exercise with my preaching students: I ask them to get up into the pulpit, and stand there. They turn their attention inward at first, feeling their feet planted on the ground, their bodies aligned and balanced, their spines long. This allows the breathing muscles to relax so that the breath can come and go freely, and drop down into the belly, where it naturally wants to go. Once they feel the breath, then they open their eyes, and breathe us in, the hearers. Then they say this simple sentence, "I am here in this room with all of you." This is a very difficult exercise. But if they can say this sentence and mean it, so that we believe it, then they can preach— or perhaps it would be better to say that they are already preaching. For in this moment they open themselves to the hearer and to God, creating a space in which God's Holy Spirit can move in and among us.

freeing the body for fuller expression

Bringing our bodies into full engagement with the moment of preaching is easier said than done. Sometimes we hear preachers and feel that their minds and spirits are communicating with us, but their bodies are asleep or shut down. Or we may feel that the preacher's words are conveying one message, but his body is saying something very different. Often I videotape my students' sermons in class, and when they watch the tape with the sound turned off, they can sometimes see that their bodies are communicating something other than what their words are saying. Physical practices such as yoga, movement, and dance can help us with this difficult task of bringing words and body more fully into alignment, so that every part of our being is contributing to the same event of communication.

Yoga developed as a practice to lead people into meditation, to ready the body in order to ready the spirit to experience stillness and silence. For this reason almost all yoga classes end in a period of rest in which the practitioner can simply be present to the moment. A central principle of yoga, then, is that physical activity must precede meditation and prayer; or, conversely, that we cannot be present in mind and spirit until our bodies become present through being warmed up, engaged, and aligned. Yoga practice leads into this stillness because it unifies the whole person—body, mind, and spirit— through the breath. In these descriptions of yoga, I am drawing on the wisdom of two yoga practitioners: Carol Wade, canon precentor at the National Cathedral, and Heather Erickson, a seminarian who has been a yoga teacher for several years. Both of them emphasize that the most important part of the yoga practice is to keep breathing while doing the yoga poses. This ongoing breath is a way of experiencing being present, no matter what is going on. Yoga also teaches us to breathe more fully, using more of our lung capacity than we usually do, and this brings us more fully into the moment.

The breath and the movement of yoga together help to achieve an integration and unity of body, mind, and spirit into the present moment. As Wade puts it, "Yoga knits me back together, so I am in my body." She describes the importance of alignment by describing how it feels to drive a car whose wheels are out of alignment: you feel the vehicle shaking and bouncing uncomfortably. When yoga brings the body back into alignment, we experience relaxation and smoothness as movement, breath, and awareness all work together. The self-conscious, judging mind becomes quiet, and there is a sense of being present without thought of a "before" or an "after." Interestingly, Erickson feels that this sense of presence arises not because she empties herself so that God can fill her, but rather because she is bringing the whole of herself into the practice and the moment. This connects with the experience of several of the preachers I interviewed, that authenticity in preaching arises not from transparency but through being fully oneself.

Both Erickson and Wade, as Christian practitioners of yoga, explicitly link yoga with central tenets of the Christian faith. Both describe yoga as an incarnational practice: just as God became flesh in Jesus Christ, so too God saves us in our bodies, and yoga is a way of experiencing God's salvation physically. For Wade, there is an explicit connection between breath and the Holy Spirit; allowing breath to enter us is allowing the Holy Spirit to dwell within us. As we recognize that our bodies are a vital part of who we are, and bring all of ourselves before God, we experience God's blessing and salvation of the whole of our beings. One aspect of the experience of blessing Wade receives from yoga is that it gives her a sense of being knit together, not only within herself, but into the body of

Christ and the communion of saints. Yoga not only integrates and aligns the individual, but integrates the individual into a larger whole.

Erickson makes a similar point by describing yoga practice in terms of *perichoresis,* a Greek word used to describe the mutually indwelling relationships among the three persons of the Trinity. The word *perichoresis* means literally "to dance around," a metaphor suggesting that the three persons of the Trinity dance with each other. As Erickson points out, this suggests a model for divine relationship that is about movement rather than words, and is circular rather than linear. Yoga is a participation in God's movement. It is also a participation in God's time; as Erickson says, the experience of being fully present in yoga practice is an experience of stepping out of temporal time, or *chronos,* into eternal time, *kairos.*

Erickson and Wade see several applications of yoga practice to preaching. Most basically, yoga practice teaches us how to be fully present, and authentic preaching relies on this sense of full and embodied presence. By learning how to bring body, mind, and spirit into alignment and engagement in the yoga studio, the preacher can bring this practice into preaching and liturgy. For instance, Wade speaks of being aware of her breathing throughout the liturgy. When she senses that her belly is tight, so that the breath cannot drop into her belly but instead is stuck in her chest, she tries to become mindful of relaxing her body and allowing the breath to travel through her once again. It is difficult to remember to breathe while preaching or leading liturgy, but if we can practice breathing while doing yoga, eventually the breath becomes so much a habit and a part of us that it becomes possible to remember the breath even in a performance situation like preaching. As with any repeated practice, the free breath eventually becomes part of us so that it is happening even when we do not notice it.

Erickson and Wade make the same point about the freedom and expressiveness of the body during preaching and worship. Preachers often feel unsure how to move their bodies, how to use gestures, and so on. Yoga takes a person through a repeated physical practice, with similar poses and movements, so that ultimately these poses and movements become part of the body's natural repertoire of expression. Over time, a repeated gesture becomes an extension of who the person is. As with the breath, the yoga practitioner becomes aware of the gesture and consciously practices it, so that when he or she is not in the yoga practice, this gesture can arise naturally. This is a specific way of talking about how the engagement and aliveness of the body that is consciously cultivated in yoga can allow the body to be more engaged and alive at other times, such as when preaching. With this engagement it more naturally and spontaneously happens that the body expresses the message of the sermon, for instance through a specific gesture, or more broadly, through the whole of the body's presence in the communication. The body's engagement in preaching and worship also leads to greater awareness of how the body is relating to the worship space, as well as to the congregation.

Wade proposes practicing movement as part of preaching preparation. She suggests "scoring the text"— that is, for each major section of the sermon, finding a physical gesture that expresses the essence of what the preacher is seeking to do in that part of the sermon. For instance, if the preacher is trying to invite hearers to some new way of looking at things, find a gesture that conveys invitation. What would the body do if it were participating in the emotion or intention of what is being communicated? It is possible to prepare a whole sermon in terms of its major physical movements, almost like creating the dance of the sermon. This dance then becomes the movement "score" that underlies the sermon when it is preached, and it may happen, quite naturally and spontaneously, that the preacher will use one of these gestures in the preaching itself. Even if this does not happen, this practice engages the body in the movement of the sermon, so the body knows what the sermon is saying, and participates in this communication.

Erickson too advocates movement as part of sermon preparation, although she proposes a more open-ended approach: simply closing the door, turning on music, and allowing your body to move and dance according to the feeling of the Scripture passage on which you are preaching. This practice allows the sermon to be formed in you physically before it finds words. Stephanie Spellers engages her body in a similar way in sermon preparation and delivery. She works on her sermons by walking and praying until the inspiration and words come, and then she types them, followed by more walking and praying. It is through this conscious bodily engagement that she finds herself in what Buddhists call the "no-mind" place, where the mind becomes settled and clear, and then she can get "synched up" with God. She integrates her body into the preaching moment itself by standing and moving around when preaching. She finds a particularly strong connection to the Spirit during the eucharistic prayer, since in this moment she is standing with arms raised, and, as is the practice at The Crossing, the other participants are joining in this gesture also.

Spellers's connection to her body in the liturgy is also greatly enhanced by music, by sensing what she calls "the groove." The groove is central to worship at The Crossing; it is the music that accompanies the service, and is played during the prayers, the eucharistic prayer, and the blessing. This music has a strong beat, and feeling this beat is crucial to Spellers's opening herself so she can become a channel. Spellers has a dance background, so for her music is always an embodied experience, and even if she does not incorporate dance practices in her preaching, "some part of me is dancing when I hear the music." Often Spellers listens and moves to music during sermon preparation, and will sing a song to begin her sermon. For Spellers, authenticity in preaching derives largely from engaging her body, from moving the sermon from her head to her body.

Two acting exercises can also help to foster the experience of discovering the movement of the text in our bodies. In the first exercise, "Group Sculptures," the instructor calls out a central word from a text, such as "comfort" from Isaiah 40:1, and one participant goes out into the center of the room and assumes a posture expressing this word. One at a time, all the other participants join the group, adding to the gesture and intensifying what the sculpture is expressing and embodying about this word. Once all have joined, everyone breathes in the feeling of the word, and then speaks the word in unison. The purpose of this exercise is to feel, physically, the meaning of the word in one's body. It is also to participate in an improvisation, since each person is adding to that which others have created, rather than planning in advance how she wants to express the word.

Another exercise, which takes this experience a step further, is called "The Dance of the Text." Participants are asked to close their eyes and stand still as the instructor reads a key phrase of a Scripture text. For instance, in John 20:11–18, the first phrase might be: "Mary stood weeping outside the tomb." The participants explore each phrase in movement, still with their eyes closed, until they find a repeating gesture that expresses their sense of the feeling of this phrase. Once they have found this gesture, the instructor reads the next key line of the text, which in John 20 might be: "She saw two angels in white." Once the group has worked its way through the text, with no more than seven key phrases, each participant will have a string of gestures that capture each key line, and these can be put together into a dance of the text. I have used this exercise with non-dancers, and have been amazed at what has emerged.

Heather Erickson and Carol Wade both feel that their knowledge of movement contributes to their understanding of the overall purpose of preaching and liturgy. Sermons are not so much about conveying doctrine, Wade says, as they are about creating an experience of God, that "incandescent moment" when heaven and earth intersect. This is a sacramental moment, in that God is made present through tangible things. Whereas in the Eucharist what is tangible is the bread and wine, in preaching the preacher's body is the tangible element, and thus it is the expressiveness of the body, as well as the words spoken, which makes God manifest.

Both Wade and Erickson argue that the great value of physically going to church, as opposed to online or televised services, is that in the former we are in a space with other bodies, and through that relationship something incarnational occurs. Erickson compares the wordless exchange occurring among bodies gathered for worship to the *perichoresis* of the Trinity, a wordless dance of conversation and exchange among selves. The practice of yoga and movement not only allow the preacher to be physically grounded in this conversation, but also to make those moment-by-moment adjustments in what she is saying and how she is saying it that are the essence of real conversation. Too often in preaching we are wedded to a prepared text, not truly open to the occasion and what it requires of us. Being physically present, however, lets us see and respond to what the moment and our hearers are offering us. This is the essence of the acting practice of improvisation, which we will discuss later in this chapter, but improvisation itself depends on physical presence in the moment.

The relationship between the preacher and the text is one of the most challenging of the preaching task. All of the preachers interviewed in chapter 3 testify in various ways that a deep engagement with Scripture is vital to good preaching, because only with such engagement can we overcome the perceived gap between the world of the text and the world to which the preacher is speaking. One excellent way to bridge this gap is by performing Scripture texts. As I argued in chapter 2, performance is helpful as a *metaphor* for preaching, and here I want to suggest that concrete *practices* of performance can also be beneficial to preachers. One that is particularly helpful is to "perform" the texts of Scripture on which you will be preaching, which means to take several steps beyond reciting it or reading it out loud. It is to learn the passage by heart, and then to act out the text as one would act out the script of a play, or to retell it as one would tell a story. To perform a passage of Scripture means to take on the voices of the characters, to stage the action, to decide what the scene looks like. While there are many excellent versions of this exercise that involve paraphrasing the text, the practice I am particularly recommending involves performing the text word for word.

As we found in chapter 2, performance practices invite us to explore the relationship between self and other through the body. Thus, performing Scripture texts is a way of experiencing the preacher-text relationship through the body and its knowledge, and bringing the text and preacher together so Scripture continues to speak to us today. Performing the text accomplishes this because the practice requires the performer to undertake a rigorous process of exegeting, interpreting, and embodying the text, and in doing so to bring his own life into relationship with the text. Preachers *should* do this, but performers *must* do it; they cannot perform without doing it, and this is why the experience of performance can deepen the practice of preaching. Performing the text compels the actor to make interpretive decisions about each word, because each word must be embodied. For instance, when Jesus says to the Syro-Phoenician woman, "It is not fair to take the children's food and throw it to the dogs" (Matt. 15:26), how does he say this line? Is he angry, sad, contemptuous, or conflicted? In order to perform a text we cannot avoid these choices, as we might in a silent reading. Because every word of the text must be embodied, we have to notice even the throwaway lines. Without interpreting the text, one cannot perform it. This is why homiletician Jana Childers says that in order "to be known, a text must be performed."[2] Having done this, the preacher is well on his way to the interpretation that leads to his sermon.

One of the tasks of actors is to make the strange familiar and the familiar strange, and as Jim Bradley noted in chapter 3, this is a task that preachers must undertake with Scripture, since this text is both too strange and too familiar. The text is strange because it speaks from a world two thousand years old, but too familiar because we have heard it many times and think we already know what it says. To perform the text—to learn it by heart, interpret it, and embody it—is to lose this easy familiarity and discover anew its strangeness and unexpectedness. The performer "reads, marks, learns, and inwardly digests it," as the collect from the *Book of Common Prayer* puts it. As the prophet Ezekiel ate the scroll and marveled at its sweetness, so too the performer takes the precious Word into her own body. As Barbara Brown Taylor says, performing Scripture is not about performing the texts "we all know" in a more lively way, but is about performing the texts none of us know unless we take them into ourselves, into our bodies, and enter into the decisions and challenges this embodied contact requires of us.[3]

In addition to making the familiar strange, the performer also makes the strange text familiar by making it deeply her own. A central principle of acting is that the truth of a text or character emerges when the performer brings her body, voice, and life experience to bear upon the text. This acting principle is related to Hans Georg Gadamer's theory of interpretation, in which he describes the process of reading a text as a conversation between the text and the reader. Understanding a text emerges when the horizon of the text meets the horizon of the reader. This means that the reader cannot understand a text if he seeks to understand it "on its own terms," for then he is denying the text's capacity to speak to his own reality. To understand a text "on its own terms" is to isolate it in the past, from which it can no longer speak; it is to imply that the text makes no claim on current experience. On the other hand, if the reader brings the fullness of his experiences into conversation with the text, he allows the text to make a claim upon him and even to change the reality he brings to the text.[4]

Performing a Scripture text means engaging in this kind of conversation with the text, in that the performer seeks to find the balance between the truth of the text and the truth that she brings to it. For instance, in performing Psalm 137, the actor must find a way to say "Happy shall they be who take your little ones and dash them against the rock!" so that these words are true for her. She must probe her own experience to discover that level of rage, despair, and lust for vengeance that would prompt her to say those words. Her own experience of these emotions is the raw material she brings to the performance of this text in order to speak it truthfully. This example, moreover, suggests that this conversation is not idle chitchat; it is passionate, intimate, and life-changing. The performer must endeavor to encounter the text at the depths from which it speaks, imprinting the text upon her own depths; "deep must call unto deep" in order for the conversation between Scripture and performer to yield the emergence of truth.

In preparing a sermon...I am hoping for a moment of revelation I can share with those who will listen to me, and I am jittery, because I never know what it may show me. I am not in control of the process. It is a process of discovery, in which I run the charged rod of God's word over the body of my own experience and wait to see where the sparks will fly.
— *Barbara Brown Taylor*

To find this meeting between the truth of the text and that of the performer is a delicate process, for it is a balance that can easily be upset in one direction or the other. An actor can overwhelm the text with his own emotion and experience, so that the text's truth no longer speaks, only the performer. On the other hand, the actor can also disappear before the text, so that he does not bring anything of his own to the encounter. We often see this during the reading of Scripture in worship, when a lector reads the lesson as though it were a foreign document, not one that he could possibly understand. In other words, we often read Scripture in church in such a way that it is not clear how it makes a claim upon us or invites us into conversation with it. I suspect that when people say of a reading of Scripture or of a sermon that "it felt like a performance," it is because this balance between text and speaker has not been found. In other words, what we call a "performance" in this negative sense is really just a *bad* performance.

This practice of performing Scripture can be used either as a part of the preacher's sermon preparation, or can become part of the liturgy itself; for instance, the text can be performed before the sermon is preached on it.

One of the preachers I interviewed, Susan Burns, was introduced to this practice when I came and directed members of her congregation in a dramatic presentation of the Passion Gospel for a Palm Sunday service. For her, the power of the event lay in the fact that it allowed the participants to "embody and become the text." Performing the text compelled them to make decisions about how to speak every word, and also how to embody it in gestures and movements. As a result, when the actors performed the text in the service, the story became so tangible that people still remember it years later. Burns subsequently adopted the practice of learning the Scripture passage by heart before preaching on it, and frequently speaks the text from memory instead of reading from the Gospel Book before preaching. The impact of this practice is to involve her on a deeper level with the text; the Word is brought close to her, so that "you have the text, and the text has you." Her own strong sense of relationship to the text is in turned shared with the congregation, who are invited in. These performance practices are one way that Burns gets "filled up with the Word" and is able to convey the sense that an encounter with God is happening right in that preaching moment.

Similarly, another seminarian who studied these performance practices with me reports that this practice has enabled him to "inhabit the experience of the gospel" when he reads the text in worship and when he preaches. Performing the Scripture passage helps him "free the text from the page." In preparing a performance of Scripture, he feels that he is called on to "use his whole self," and to "pull wisdom from his deepest self," so as to understand on a deep and personal level what the text is saying. This kind of understanding is necessary in order to perform the text truthfully.

Performing Scripture texts is a helpful practice for preachers because it is a way of fostering intimacy with a chosen passage, encouraging deeper listening and speaking. It is one way to "submit to the text," as Ellen Davis would say, and to enter the story of the text, as Mariann Budde describes it. This deep relationship arises out of the engagement of the preacher's own body with the text in addition to the mind and spirit. When we allow ourselves to tap into the body's wisdom about a text, then a bridge is formed and a connection made between the world of the text and our world today. As a preacher allows the text to live in his body while performing it, he also make the connections, physical and spiritual, that allow the sermon that arises out of the text to live in his body as well. Once this embodied connection between self and text is made during the performance of the text, the preacher can draw on this same living relationship while preaching.

---

improvisation in preaching

Improvisation can be a very helpful discipline for the preacher to learn, one that can assist greatly in her ability to be both authentic and authoritative. The word "improvisation," like the word "performance," can have negative connotations, however, so it is important to address these at the outset. Studying the practice of improvisation as a preacher does not mean deciding that we are no longer going to prepare our sermons ahead of time, but rather choosing to stand up and preach whatever the Spirit (or our own egos, or our own current obsessions) tells us to say in that moment. Preaching that honors the relationships that make up the preaching moment—with self, God, text, tradition, and hearers—requires spending time in rigorous study of all of these conversation partners. Certainly all of our preachers in the previous chapter advocate careful study of Scripture, thoughtful application of the Scripture to the situation of the congregation, and a deep exploration of self in relationship to God. All of these must be done ahead of time and brought to that moment. For this reason, some homileticians object to practices of improvisation for preachers since it may encourage them (especially beginners) to feel that they can dispense with rigorous preparation—a temptation that will be plenty strong enough in the midst of a busy pastor's life.

[We are] victimized by...the deadening force of words that are no longer enfleshed or carry meaning...the fear of telling the truth about one's experience.... *Getting things right.* These are pitfalls of religious writing and they are pitfalls of church practice.
— *Nora Gallagher*

Practices of improvisation are not about teaching pastors to preach on the spur of the moment, but involve learning how to be more fully present and responsive to the moment and its demands. As Jim Bradley and our other preachers have suggested, openness and responsiveness are fundamental to the preaching task. In some cases, actual interruptions will happen during the sermon itself—a screaming infant, a fire truck going by or, as in Bradley's case, a member of the congregation asking a question in the middle of the sermon. Even without interruptions, however, it is still true that preaching is a back-and-forth conversation and thus we as preachers have to be open to that conversation evolving and taking directions we had not anticipated. When this happens, how can we respond to what we are receiving and still keep the conversation flowing? In these cases having a well-prepared text may actually get in our way, because it focuses us on *getting through* what we have written, rather than on what is happening in the room at that very moment. This is where practices of improvisation can be crucially helpful, teaching us how to sense and respond in the moment of preaching no matter how risky that may seem.

In reflecting on the value of improvisation for preaching, I have been helped by the work of Samuel Wells, whose book *Improvisation: The Drama of Christian Ethics* sets forth the practice and theory of improvisation as a central metaphor for the Christian life.[5] It is important to note that Wells objects to improvisation being seen *only* in relationship to the practice of preaching, since he feels it can helpfully inform Christian ethical existence as a whole. He argues that the Christian life can be seen as a performance of the truths found in Scripture, such that the life and practices of the believing community are a living enactment of the Christian faith. However, to call such enactment "performance" is a distortion of its meaning, Wells maintains, for this suggests that the Christian life is about following a predetermined script. In fact, what Christians need to be able to do is to know how to act ethically when confronted with new circumstances. This is where the practice of improvisation, as studied in the theater, can be helpful. It is not about spontaneity leading to chaos, but about being schooled so deeply in the church's tradition that when some new situation comes along, the Christian already knows how to behave in that moment. Conceiving of the Christian life as improvisation, as Wells does, means that Christians live within a framework that is so much a part of them that when the moment for moral decision and action arises, they know instinctively how to respond.

How does this concept of improvisation help us with the preaching task? Let us take a concrete example of an improvisation exercise that I use in my preaching classes, which I call "Building the Story." A person stands up and begins to tell a story; whenever he chooses he can ask, "What happens next?" Then someone else in the group has to jump up and continue the story, until that person in turn asks, "What happens next?" and then the next person jumps in.

This exercise leads to another exercise more specifically concerned with preaching, called "Group Sermon." Here the instructor reads a Scripture text, one the students have not been given in advance, and then immediately someone begins the sermon. This person can either open it to someone else by saying, "What comes next?" or if someone listening feels so moved, she can interrupt the speaker and continue the sermon, at which point the first person sits down. This goes on until someone decides that the sermon is done. Almost invariably, when this exercise is working well, the entire group has a clear, almost visceral sense of when the sermon is complete.

One of the most important lessons to learn from improvisation exercises like these is the practice of "accepting" rather than "blocking." To accept is to receive freely whatever your improvisation partners do, and work within these conditions. To "block" is to refuse what they have created, thus undermining what they have given rather than working with it. To do this is to kill off the story or the sermon that is being developed by the group. The group sermon works only if each person who adds to it accepts the givens others have created, and builds on them, rather than rejecting them by taking the sermon in a different direction. The group sermon is seriously impaired when a participant decides not to continue the course being developed but instead to take the sermon in another direction, which may have more to do with her assumption about what the biblical text means than with listening to the wisdom of the group. As Wells says, improvisation is not about being "original," but about making the "obvious" choice, building on all that has preceded that moment. Similarly, improvisation is not about individuals being clever, but about a community developing such trust in one another that they can cooperate effortlessly.

What this exercise gives preachers is a profound experience of the truly conversational nature of preaching, and an ability to build on the conversation that is always going on between preacher and hearers. Through exercises like the Group Sermon, preachers learn how to be attentive to the voice of the congregation and responsive to it in the moment, rather than clinging too rigidly to their own sense of what needs to be said in the sermon. This experience has clear applications in moments of interruption in the sermon, when the preacher needs to know how to respond, but it is also helpful throughout the sermon, since he always needs to listen deeply to the congregation even while he is speaking to them. These exercises teach the preacher to approach the preaching event in an attitude of *accepting* whatever the moment brings, under whatever conditions the congregation, the setting, or the season offer. As Wells points out, we usually block out the input of others when it seems "improper, impossible, or dangerous"; but improvisation teaches us to regard nothing in this light, but to accept and work with everything that occurs, for nothing is outside of the reach of God's grace.[6]

This exercise, and others like it, also teach preachers the all-important lesson of trusting what is in us and what God has given us to say. This is the great value of improvisation, as Wells sees it: that Christians, having been schooled in the habits and traditions of the faith, will know the right thing to do at the right moment. This aptitude comes both from deep schooling in the Christian faith and life, forming habits that one falls back on in moments of uncertainty, and also from an ability to trust oneself and to trust God. It means not only accepting and building on what the group has created, but also trusting our instinct rather than seeking to be "original." As Keith

Johnstone, the author of a well-known manual on theatrical improvisation, writes:

> People trying to be original always arrive at the same boring old answers. Ask people to give you an original idea and see the chaos it throws them into. If they said the first thing that came into their head, there'd be no problem. An artist who is inspired is being *obvious*. He's not making decisions, he's not weighing up one idea against another.[7]

Being "obvious" is trusting and tapping into what a preacher knows to be true, what God has given to that preacher and lives inside of her.

Sometimes at the beginning of an introductory preaching class, I will ask students to stand up and preach a completely improvised sermon, without any prior preparation. This exercise usually has fantastic results, for students are amazed to discover that they *do* have something to say, that they have preachers' hearts and voices within themselves. This exercise not only builds confidence, it gives them the experience of trusting themselves in the moment to say the right thing. What is happening in this moment is not pure spontaneity, but rather spontaneity that emerges out of long habits and training in the Christian life. As Jim Bradley notes, his air of spontaneity in preaching and leading worship is founded on years of living and preaching the Christian life; it has taught him how to act and react in any given circumstance. Although beginning preachers do not have this depth of experience, they still have been formed in the Christian faith over many years, and thus are more capable of bearing spontaneous witness to this faith than they realize.

One thing that frightens people about delivering an improvised sermon is not so much that they have *nothing* to say, but rather that they will say the *wrong* thing, something "heretical" or worse, something that taps into an unsavory part of their own characters that they would rather not have others know about. Speaking and responding in an unplanned way means tapping into instinct and the unconscious, and we are often afraid of what is lurking in these parts of our being. One improvisation exercise that illustrates this is the "Word at a Time" game, in which a group constructs a story by each person adding a word, going around in a circle. In order for the story to work, participants need to say the first thing that comes into their heads, without stopping to think about it. Often it happens that the story quickly becomes improper or even obscene, since these may be the first things to come into our heads. In Carl Jung's terminology, our "shadow" is becoming visible, those parts of ourselves that we normally hide and suppress.

> I also had the distinct and painful sensation that every time I got up to preach, I was leaving parts of myself behind. In Harry Potter lingo, the term for that is *splinching,* "the separation of random body parts," and it occurs when a wizard-in-transit loses focus and concentration and inadvertently leaves a leg or an ear behind. Splinching is not pretty to watch or to experience. When moving from one place to another, the goal is to arrive whole and intact; no one wants to lose heart or mind or guts on the way to the pulpit.
> — *Anna Carter Florence*

As preachers, we may well feel that our "shadow" has no place in preaching the "Good News," and that we do not want to engage in any practice that gives permission for that shadow side to show itself or to speak. However, if being fully present and authentic in preaching is really about integrating all of ourselves into the preaching event, then somehow our shadow has to be integrated as well. If we do not do this, then we essentially preach in a state of fearing ourselves, needing to keep the lid on an unruly mess within, all of which leads to fragmentation and lack of presence. Ironically, this kind of repression often leads to situations where the suppressed shadow asserts itself in very inappropriate ways. One benefit of improvisation, therefore, is that it acquaints us with our shadow in a way that allows it to be redeemed and fully integrated. As Wells puts it, "By articulating the unconscious, improvisation opens the Christian community up to grace: it does not bury its unknown gift, but trades with it, and thus comes to know it, and to trust God to forgive and heal it when necessary."[8]

Another value of improvisation is that it teaches us the importance of play in Christian life, ministry, and preaching. Indeed, we may be suspicious of improvisation because it is playful, and that may seem to suggest that it is trivial and self-indulgent. But play is crucial to Christian life and preaching. Play involves a suspension of goal-oriented patterns of thought and behavior, since it is undertaken only for its own sake. It is a time of exploration and experimentation that gives the imagination free rein. It is open space, and those who enter it do not need a purpose for their actions beyond the joy of play itself. And play is often about the inversion of normal rules of behaving and thinking, such as when my three-year-old son says, "Pretend I'm the Mommy, and you're the baby," and we enter the game from this premise. Similarly, during a recent course on preaching the Gospel of John, at various points my co-teacher and I drew people into improvised retellings of the text from different perspectives. For instance, we asked them to improvise the meeting between Jesus and the woman at the well as a meeting at a bar, the raising of Lazarus as soap opera or melodrama, and the trial of Jesus before Pilate as a scene from a western movie.[9]

As we discovered in these exercises, entering this space of play has several benefits for preachers. First of all, it is an invitation to spend time in God's already redeemed cosmos which has ample time for joy and pleasure, because in God's reign nothing needs to be fixed or accomplished. For preachers to spend time in this kingdom is to remember that the ultimate purpose of our preaching is to herald this reign, and invite people into it. Second, as we learned in replaying John's Gospel in different modes, free play unlocks the imagination, the soul, and the unconscious, all of which need to enter into any kind of creative activity, including preaching. This is particularly necessary in reading Scripture, since we tend to get locked into conventional and narrow ways of reading the text, whereas play can free our minds to look at the text differently. Third, entering a space where normal rules are reversed reminds us that God's kingdom always involves profound reversals, in which the first shall be last and that last shall be first. Finally, our fear of preaching, and the seriousness with which we take it, can lead to a deadly solemnity in our preaching, which stems from taking ourselves too seriously. We forget that we are doing this with God, not by ourselves, and so we can have a sense of lightness and joy in this vocation. The practice of play can remind us to take ourselves less seriously, and to allow the joy of God's presence to leaven our preaching.

Stephanie Spellers's descriptions of using improvisation in her ministry provide a concrete example of the value and lessons of improvisation that we have been sketching here. She improvises not during the sermon but during other parts of the worship service at The Crossing: the welcome, the eucharistic prayer, and the closing blessing. Because these parts of the service are delivered extemporaneously, she needs to listen more deeply to the congregation and all aspects of the liturgy, so as to articulate in these parts of the service what the moment requires. She practices "accepting" what is happening and building on it, rather than "blocking" it in order to say what she meant to say all along. The decision to speak these parts of the service extemporaneously compels her to "throw the door open" to God, asking God to work in and through her in that moment. She has learned to trust God, and what God has given her to say in that moment, something she finds harder to do when delivering a sermon prepared ahead of time. In the improvised portions of the service, Spellers experiences the kind of openness and non-defensiveness that improvisation teaches and requires, and this openness allows the Spirit to work through her powerfully.

The ability of an improviser to accept rather than block, to respond in the moment to what is being given, to trust his own instinct, to become acquainted with his own shadow, and to play all depends on being able to enter a state of what Wells calls "relaxed awareness." This is a state of readiness and alertness, in which "the actor senses no need to impose an order on the outside world or on the imagination; there is an openness to receiving and giving. The actor is at one with the whole context: self, other actors, audience, theater space."[10] This state is similar to the state of presence that we explored in chapter 2, and is a primary goal of Linklater's voice work, as well as of yoga and movement. Improvisation, like these other practices, teaches us how to be present in the moment, and how to respond to whatever happens without defensiveness or fear. As preachers we have reasons to be defensive, because ours is a high calling. We have an important and complex tradition to pass on, and we are very much on display and open to judgment in doing what we do. Improvisation teaches us, however, that we do not need to defend either ourselves or our tradition, no matter what the moment throws at us. As preachers we have reasons to be afraid, because preaching calls us to be open to God, self, and congregation in deep and sometimes frightening ways. However, improvisation teaches us how to move beyond our fears; rather than "blocking" what the preaching moment offers, we can be open to the Spirit and face the unknown without fear.

I have been arguing that the preacher's authenticity and authority in her relationships with text, congregation, God, and self depend on a kind of presence that is holistic: a presence not only in mind and spirit, but also in body. A basic premise of this book is that this kind of presence can actually be learned through very concrete practices. While there are numerous spiritual practices and habits of mind that can foster this ability to be present, one of the best ways to develop this sense of presence is through practices that engage our bodies. Working with our bodies teaches us that a sense of presence is not an abstraction but a concrete matter of physical alignment, breath, and voice. We can fool ourselves as to whether our spirits are present or not, but there is no mistaking when our bodies are tuned into the moment and when they are not. By the same token, if we feel we are not present, the spiritual adjustment may be difficult to make in the moment. However, if we can breathe, if we can stand with both feet on the ground, we are taking concrete steps to show up more fully.

If we are seeking an authentic and authoritative presence in preaching, it makes sense to start with specific practices that bring our bodies, as well as the rest of ourselves, into the room and the moment. What Linklater's voice work, yoga and movement, performing Scripture texts, and improvisation have in common is that they are all practices that deliberately awaken and engage the body. Thus preachers can learn in an immediate, visceral way what it takes to be present, and how to do this in their preaching.

I have focused on physical practices in this chapter not only because they offer concrete ways of becoming more fully present in preaching. I also chose this emphasis because, although preaching is clearly an embodied activity, we do not focus as much attention on training the body for preaching as we do on instructing the mind and spirit. It is as though we work *around* our bodies in our preaching, rather than with and through them. The fact that we have ignored, discounted, or suppressed our bodies' presence and wisdom is one of the primary causes of inauthenticity in preaching today. In order to address this strange blindness to our physical being, it is important that we engage it directly. Through bringing the body as well as the mind and spirit to preaching, we discover a full presence that is a foundation of authenticity and authority in our preaching.

chapter five

The Adventure of the Word Made Flesh

> On the whole, I do not find Christians, outside of the
> catacombs, sufficiently sensible of conditions. Does anyone
> have the foggiest idea what sort of power we blindly
> invoke? Or, as I suspect, does no one believe a word of it?
> The churches are children playing on the floor with their
> chemistry sets, mixing up a batch of TNT to kill a Sunday
> morning. It is madness to wear ladies' straw hats and
> velvet hats to church; we should all be wearing crash
> helmets. Ushers should issue life preservers and signal
> flares; they should lash us to our pews. For the sleeping god
> may wake someday and take offense, or the waking god
> may draw us out to where we can never return.
> —Annie Dillard

Suppose Tom, a visitor, walked into the Church of the
Holy Spirit, a church whose preachers followed the
principles and practices I have been describing in this
book. What might he see and experience? As I spin out
this fantasy scenario of transformed and transformational
preaching, it will become evident that I am borrowing

some ideas and practices from the preachers I interviewed, perhaps most especially the emergent church practices of The Crossing, as well as adding some of my own emphases.

When Tom first walks in, he is struck by the space: the sanctuary is in a traditional church building, but it has no fixed pews, but instead has chairs that can be moved. The chairs are set up in a horseshoe for today's service. There is space around the chairs, in front and behind them, and he notices exercise mats spread out on some of the floor space. There is an altar and a simple pulpit in the open part of the horseshoe.

He sits down and the service begins. When it comes time for the reading of Scripture prior to the sermon, someone steps up to the front and invites the congregation to stand and do a simple stretching exercise. They stretch their arms straight over their heads, stretching up all the way through their fingertips, then drop over slowly until they are hanging head downwards, then uncurl up. After it is over Tom realizes that he is feeling more awake, more able to listen to whatever will come next. Looking around, he sees that all the others look a bit more present, more plugged in, as well. Then comes his next big surprise: someone walks over to the pulpit, picks up the large open Bible resting there, says, "The Holy Gospel according to Mark," but then puts the book down and comes and stands in the horseshoe among the people, and begins to speak the text from memory. It is the story in the Gospel of Mark about the healing of the Gerasene demoniac (Mark 5:1–20), and the speaker does not so much act it out as tell it like a story, though still using only the words from the Scripture. He conveys the voices of the different characters—the harrowing shrieks of the demoniac, the power of Jesus' words, the fearfulness of the townspeople coming to see what has happened. Mainly he tells the story with his voice, though he adds a few movements and gestures here and there, most strikingly at the end when he kneels as the healed man to beg Jesus to take him along with the other disciples. Tom is struck by how real the story suddenly feels, as though he were right there on the hillside watching it all unfold.

After this performance, the preacher moves to the pulpit to begin the sermon. She is not vested as a priest, so Tom cannot tell if she is ordained or not. When she arrives at the pulpit, she stands for a moment in silence, then invites the congregation to take a moment to center themselves and to breathe. There is a minute when the whole congregation simply breathes together, while the preacher stands and looks at them while they look at her. There is an amazing feeling in that silence before any words are spoken—a deep sense of anticipation, an expectation that something miraculous is going to emerge from within and beyond them. It is like the silence of a full orchestra before the first note of the symphony is played. There is a sense of this whole community being gathered into one, as though they are all stepping onto a boat that is going to take them out over unknown waters. They let the boat stop rocking before the preacher pushes the boat off the sand and into the deep. Suddenly it seems to Tom that this moment might be the most beautiful sermon he has ever heard; that nothing needs to be said that could be more lovely and nourishing than this deep, and deeply shared, silence.

But then the preacher begins the sermon. Immediately Tom is struck by something intangible but very real in the quality of her presence. *I feel like she is really here with us, really talking to us, not* at us, *like so many preachers I have heard,* Tom thinks. She has a lot to say, but for some reason she does not seem preachy. The way she stands makes Tom feel she is at home and alive in her body. He wonders if the exercise they did before the sermon began has something to do with this sense of aliveness. Tom is also struck by her words—they are not just words, but real somehow. They really mean something. *It's like I can see and feel what she is talking about as she speaks,* Tom thinks. *There's a passion and commitment that come through in her speaking that make me want to listen.* Tom looks around, and notices that everyone around him is also listening—listening as though she is speaking for them. Whenever she pauses, it seems like they are breathing with her; it's almost like they are feeding her the words she is saying. Another extraordinary thing: she is not using a microphone, yet her voice fills the space, which is big!

It is the privilege of the preacher to orient people toward mystery, to lead them close enough to be touched by it. That is a priestly privilege, whether or not the preacher is formally ordained. And one thing that is evident from the biblical representation of priesthood is that it is a role that involves measured speaking; the presence of mystery reveals the foolishness of "trite, hackneyed Christian chatter" (Gerhard von Rad). — *Ellen F. Davis*

Tom notices that the preacher engages Scripture deeply and thoughtfully, as though she has truly allowed it to speak to and transform her, and as though she has thought about how it could transform this community as well. Her words are clearly personal for her, even though she does not tell a personal story. He suspects that the most personal part for her comes when she is talking about why the healed demoniac wanted to go with Jesus at the end, and why Jesus refused and told him to stay and preach to his own people. This is the same moment that the gospel performer made so dramatic in his presentation of the text before the sermon began. Tom wonders if the two of them worked on this together. It's right at this moment, when deep emotion suffuses the preacher's voice and presence, and some profound personal experience seems to fuel her words, that Tom gets the strangest feeling of all: a kind of electric sensation that shoots through him and, he is sure, through the others there. It's as though they are all being borne up and held together in a hand, a presence, that goes beyond any of them. It feels for a moment that a door has opened and drawn them into a different kind of time, which might last forever.

After the preacher has spoken for ten minutes or so, she stops speaking and goes to sit in front of the pulpit. At first Tom thinks the sermon is over, but then he is surprised again: someone near him stands and speaks about the text and what the preacher has said, continuing the sermon. Several more people stand and add to what has been said, sometimes referring to the preacher's words, and sometimes to the performer's presentation of the text. After each contribution that wonderful listening, breathing silence picks up again, like a rich chord sustaining a piece of music.

At first Tom wonders if all these people have worked out their comments ahead of time, because they build on each other in an almost seamless way. In addition, these speakers seem to know this text as well as the performer and preacher did, and he notices that their words have that same fullness of meaning these two speakers' words had. But despite what appears like deep preparation and attunement, their words feel so spontaneous that he concludes there is no way they could have been prepared beforehand. These contributions feel different from the first preacher's words, which, even though she was very present, did seem well thought-out beforehand. Then his hunch is verified, when one of the speakers begins by saying, "I'm surprised to be talking right now—but the Spirit moved me in what you just said." But if this sermon time is not planned, how will they know when to end it,

Tom wonders? Yet right as he's thinking this, there's a comment that seems to sum up everything in an astonishing way. "Amen," he finds himself saying out loud in response. And then there's another silence—but this time like something settling, or like the boat they are all in easing back onto the sandy beach and coming to rest. They wait until it stops rocking; then someone else stands and says, "Let us pray."

I need to find out more about this, Tom decides, because I have never experienced preaching that felt this way. So after the sermon he finds the preacher and asks her: "Where did that come from? What was that moment we all felt during the sermon? How did you make that happen? How did everyone know what to say? How did I know to say 'Amen'?"

She laughs and says, "Well, it didn't come out of nowhere, so it will take a bit of time to explain what we do to support the preaching here. And I should warn you that even all that we do does not 'make' moments like that happen. That's the Spirit's work. But there are many things we do to prepare for the Spirit to show up."

the preacher's rule of life

"The first thing we do," the preacher continues, "is really an attitude: we take preaching very seriously around here. We think of it as one of the most precious things we do together. After all, this practice has been handed down to us through the church since the time of the Hebrew prophets. They really believed that God could speak through their human words, and we really believe that God can show up and speak in our words. We believe that the Word can become flesh and dwell among us. So preaching is a time and space set apart from all others in which we truly hope and expect that God will be with us and speak to us. And of course that's what we all want more than anything else—to know God, to feel God's presence, to experience God's love.

"And we think that is what God most wants too—to know us and be close to us. So we protect the sacred space of preaching because this is where we believe that we can find this, our hearts' desire and God's desire. What is important is that we all protect this space together, that everyone here is responsible for tending this practice and keeping it strong and healthy, just like everyone cares for a common garden or community well. Every member of this congregation is always preparing to preach. This is part of the commitment that each new member makes when he or she joins this church. The way we organize the worship space reflects the way we think about preaching: the chairs are in a horseshoe so everyone present can see and interact with each other, because we hold preaching together; but the circle is open, because we are hoping and expecting to receive something divine that breaks in from outside our circle.

"There are several practices we do here, outside of the preaching moment itself, that are part of our constant preparation. These practices are open to all members and visitors, but certain members commit to doing them regularly. They take on, in a sense, 'the preacher's rule of life.' This group is called 'The Preaching Leaveners,' after that passage in Scripture where the woman hid a bit of leaven in the bread dough and it raised the whole loaf. So this core group is the preaching leaven that gives life and nourishment to all of the preaching we do here. It is from this group of Leaveners that the preachers are chosen who begin the sermon, as I did today. The idea is that you have to have taken on this rule of life and be doing these practices in order to be the main preacher of the day. This is a sign of how seriously we take preaching. But the others who spoke after me don't have to be part of this group of

Leaveners, although they are welcome to do any of the practices with us, and can join the Leaveners at any time, as long as they take on the rule of life that we are doing. Taking on this rule of life, rather than being ordained, is the requirement for being a Leavener and a lead preacher here.

"So what is the preacher's rule of life? The first part of it is Scripture study: deep engagement and wrestling with the Bible. There are ongoing Bible study groups here, and each week a group gathers to consider the text for the upcoming Sunday. Whoever is preaching on that Sunday commits to going to that study group that is discussing the text on which he is going to preach. The performer of the Scripture passage also has to be part of that study group. It's important that part of this study process involves consulting with commentaries, doing word study and other exegetical work. Those with theological education teach us how to do this and help us find the scholarly resources to use, and we are committed to using them as we get ready to preach. The point is that Scripture needs to be studied, and needs to be central to the sermon, not just a jumping off point for whatever I or someone else might want to say. As you saw in the things people said after I finished speaking, people come to know the Bible pretty well around here! Along with this Scripture study there needs to be self-examination and spiritual discernment, so we really hear what this text is saying to *our* lives.

"But all this study and preparation is not just about engaging our heads and our spirits. You may have noticed the stretching exercise we did before the Scripture, and the invitation to breathe before the sermon. Or you may have noticed that our voices were strong enough to fill the space without microphones. Or you may have noticed a sense of presence and aliveness in our voices and bodies. These are giveaways to a whole other set of practices we do here. We believe that if we are preparing for the Word to become flesh, we need to engage our flesh also as we get ready.

"Preaching happens in our bodies and voices, right? So we feel we should tune our bodies and voices so they can do this as well as possible—just as you wouldn't go out and figure skate in the Olympics without practicing your jumps and spins over and over. We learn how to use our voices so that they can convey the full thought and feeling we want to express. This practice of training the voice takes a long time and a big commitment, but you can make a lot of progress in the ten-week voice class we have here each year.

"We have classes too in yoga and movement, so that our bodies can learn how to preach as well. We push the chairs in the sanctuary back against the walls, and we have a beautiful dance space there. Many people think dance, movement, and yoga are only for a select few, but actually you'd be surprised at how accessible these can be—as you can see from that stretch we did in the service today. We find that these classes really become opportunities for spiritual development, as well as community-building. Anyone can take them, but the Leaveners need to take both a voice class and a movement/yoga class before they can preach. We try to incorporate both practices into the worship itself, which is why we do a simple movement exercise before the sermon, and try to incorporate our voice training when we speak.

"What makes the voice work and the movement classes work so well together is that they are both based on learning how to breathe. If you learn how to breathe the way you did when you were a baby, where it's your whole body breathing, then everything else about preaching is secondary. I know that sounds too simplistic, but it is true, because the breath in us is God's Spirit in us. When we let ourselves breathe, we let God in—and remember, that's what preaching is for, right—to let God become present among us? But the tragic thing is that we have forgotten how to breathe, and we have to learn it all over again. Now I *know* this is going to sound crazy, but a lot of our work here in this congregation is learning how to breathe. We firmly believe that if we can learn to breathe again, and breathe together, and keep breathing no matter what, that not only will God be made known among us again and again, but also the world itself will be changed. Okay, that sounds far-fetched, but think about how that shared breath in the silence felt today—like we were all together, like we hardly needed words at all. It's because we care so much about the breath, in fact, that we named this community the Church of the Holy Spirit.

"One way we put together these two parts of our preparation—Scripture study and voice and body training—is in performing the Scripture passage before the sermon. The idea here is that we need to bring the Scripture passage right into our bodies so that it becomes part of us. It makes the story so immediate, so relevant. That in itself is the Word becoming flesh and dwelling among us, and sometimes a performance will be so profound there's almost no need for a sermon afterward. Also, as the preacher is preparing the sermon, he or she works with the performer. The performer gives feedback on the preacher's sermon, and the preacher gives feedback on the performer's presentation of the text. This way there is some consistency in their interpretations of the passage, though they don't have to be in total agreement. You probably noticed that both the performer and I today focused on the last part of that Mark story, where Jesus tells the healed man to go and proclaim what has happened to him. As we were working on the sermon, we felt that this was the part of the passage that was most important for both of us, and for the community—partly because it is about preaching!

"Now I haven't even told you about my favorite practice of all that we do to prepare for preaching, and that is Improv Class. It's just so fun! But there is a serious purpose to it also. We figure that if we are going to open up preaching so that everyone is invited to offer their own reflections after the main sermon, then we need to practice ahead of time in order to do this well. Once you become a grown-up, you have to learn how to be spontaneous! What we need to practice is how to listen to each other, how to be open to what the other person is saying, so whatever we feel moved to say builds on what everyone has said before. So it's not about just sitting there thinking about what you want to say, and waiting until the other person has stopped talking so you can say your bit. It's about taking in what everyone is saying, and then listening to the Spirit's prompting as to how you can join in and add to what is being developed by the group. Improvisation exercises teach all of this; some of them are pretty goofy—like let's all tell a story one word at a time— but they teach us how to create something together, instead of being each on our own wavelengths. You'd be surprised at how this even helps us in vestry meetings! Once again, each Leavener has to take one of our improvisation classes before they can preach, but anyone can take a class, and they are very popular.

"You know, I have to admit that preaching really is frightening; it's always been so for me, and probably always will be. But what we have decided here at the Church of the Holy Spirit is—let's have preaching be terrifying for the *right* reasons, not the *wrong* reasons. Let's let preaching be scary not because you feel all alone when you preach, or you feel that everyone is judging you, but because we are handling the Word of God, and that Word is dangerous. Annie Dillard said that if we really believed what we were saying in church, we ought to show up with crash helmets, because God coming among us really is that frightening. But instead we do everything we can to keep God from entering into our worship. Sometimes when I listen to preachers I feel like they are trying as hard as possible to get through their sermons without the Spirit showing up and messing with them. That's what makes preaching 'preachy': when someone gives you all the answers *about* God while keeping all the doors *to* God firmly shut—papering over our fear of ourselves, the world, the unknown, and the divine with platitudes. Okay, the Spirit is dangerous, and frightening, but she is also the breath of life! So we here are trying to make space for her to appear, and that's what all these practices are about, and what we are trying to do in our preaching. Let's hold the terror and joy of preaching *together as a community,* and not make one person hold it all alone. And let's learn practices that help us work with our fear, so we can be open to what God wants to do in preaching. Preaching should be a risky and glorious gallop, not a limp trot through clichés—so safe, boring, predictable, and lifeless! No, no—bring out the crash helmets, and let God's Word happen!

"I should tell you that you don't have to take any of these classes—in Scripture study, voice, movement, or improvisation—in order to contribute to the sermon, as you did today. But we've learned that if there's a critical mass of people in the congregation who are steeped in these practices, then that is enough to create the tone of the service and make the sermon work. Again, it's like the leaven in the dough; those who have practiced and studied raise preaching to a new level for everyone, and even visitors like yourself feel inspired by it. Then sometimes those visitors decide they don't want to be visitors any more, but want to join us in this adventure of the Word becoming flesh: so how about you, preacher?"

A Guide for Discussion

You may of course read the books in this series on your own, but because they focus on the transformation of the Episcopal Church in the twenty-first century, the books are especially useful as a basis for discussion and reflection within a congregation or community. The questions below are intended to generate fruitful discussion about the congregations with which members of the group are familiar.

Each group will identify its own needs and will be shaped by the interests of the participants and their comfort in sharing personal life stories. Discussion leaders will wish to focus on particular areas that address the concerns and goals of the group, using the questions and themes provided here simply as suggestions for a place to start the conversation.

chapter one

Why Is It Frightening to Preach?

In this chapter Ruthanna Hooke notes that fear of preaching is a common—and perhaps realistic and healthy—response from those who attempt to preach.

* What is your experience of preaching? When do you look forward to hearing or preaching the sermon? When do you dread it? Why?

* How do the feelings of the preacher toward preaching manifest themselves during a sermon? How do they affect the ability of the listeners to hear?

* What are some of the signs of authenticity you look for in a preacher?

◆　◆　◆　◆　◆

The author asks the question: "If preaching is part of God's self-revelation and a transforming encounter with God's own Word, what is the role of the preacher in this event?" (p. 8).

* How would you answer her question?

* Describe some of the preachers you have known throughout your life whose sermons or way of preaching have informed your sense of what the role of the preacher can be (or should not be).

* How would you describe the role of the hearers in the event of preaching?

chapter two

"Is There a Word from the Lord?"

In this chapter the author states: "Although all aspects of life can be occasions for encountering God, preaching is believed to be privileged, just as the sacraments are. This is why, in some churches, listeners approach the sermon not so much with the question, 'What does the preacher have to say today?' but rather with the question, 'Is there a Word from the Lord?'" (p. 24).

- ◆ Do you come to sermons, either as a preacher or a hearer, expecting a Word from the Lord? Why or why not? What would it sound like? How would you know it is "from the Lord"?

- ◆ With what other questions do you and others in your congregation approach the sermon? What are you seeking?

- ◆ When have you heard or given a sermon that you thought was truly "inspired," or filled with the Holy Spirit? What was different about that preaching experience?

◆   ◆   ◆   ◆   ◆

In speaking about the physical dimension of preaching, the author notes, "Both the doctrine of the Incarnation and the metaphor of performance urge us to be present in our full humanity when we preach. This means being present in body as well as in mind and spirit" (p. 37).

- ◆ How would you respond to the questions on pages 37 and 39–40 about the embodiment of preaching in your congregation?

- ◆ Now consider the questions on pages 40–41 about the way preaching reflects—or does not reflect—our beliefs about God and the church. How would preaching need to change in your congregation to be more in alignment with your experience of God?

♦ What do you think are the foundations of authenticity and authority in preaching?

<hr>

chapter three

Profiles of Preachers

In this chapter Ruthanna Hooke explores the preaching practices of eight experienced preachers in the Episcopal Church.

♦ What common themes in philosophy and practices of preaching do you see in these eight preachers?

♦ What strikes you as the most helpful insights they share about how they approach the preaching task?

♦   ♦   ♦   ♦   ♦

For the author these profiles raise three essential questions about preaching the church today:

♦ What tools can preachers use to help them engage more deeply and powerfully in their relationships with Scripture, God, congregation, and self?

♦ How can preachers make themselves more open to God and the congregation so that preaching becomes a conversation among these three parties?

♦ What practices can help preachers discover the appropriate balance between self and role, between private self and public *persona*? (pp. 46–47)

With these three questions in mind, develop a written profile of yourself as a preacher. If possible, share your profile with a trusted colleague or in a small group, as appropriate.

If you are not a preacher, develop a profile of the relationship of preacher and hearers in your congregation, from the perspective of the congregation as an active participant in the preaching event.

chapter four

Engaging the Body in Preaching

In this chapter the author explores four concrete practices involving the body as a way of "bringing the whole self more fully to the preaching moment, finding the presence of God in the preaching moment, feeling the truth of the text in our bodies and voices, and connecting to the congregation" (p. 97).

♦ Reflect on the importance of the voice in preaching in your congregation. When have you been aware of the preacher's voice as conveying a sense of authenticity?

♦ Try the exercise the author does with her students, described on page 102. (If a pulpit is not available, use another suitable space in the room.) What did you learn from this exercise?

♦ ♦ ♦ ♦ ♦

♦ Reflect on what is (or is not) communicated by the preacher's body and the bodies of listeners during the preaching event in your congregation.

+ Try one of the two acting exercises—"Group Sculptures" and "The Dance of the Text"—described on pages 108–109. What did you learn?

◆　◆　◆　◆　◆

+ What is your experience of seeing Scripture performed? How was it different from simply hearing the passage read aloud?

+ Choose a passage from Scripture and try performing it, either alone or in small groups.

◆　◆　◆　◆　◆

+ When is room provided for improvisation in your congregation's worship or preaching? How comfortable is the congregation with the need to improvise when the unexpected happens?

+ Try the "Building the Story" or "Group Sermon" exercises described on pages 117–118. What did you learn from that experience?

chapter five

The Adventure of the
Word Made Flesh

In this chapter the author offers a "fantasy scenario of transformed and transformational preaching" (p. 127) at the Church of the Holy Spirit.

+ Would you like to become a member of the Church of the Holy Spirit? Why or why not?

+ In what ways does the Church of the Holy Spirit resemble your own congregation? How does it differ?

⬥ Who are the individuals who function as "Preaching Leaveners" in your congregation now? In other words, who helps to guide the preacher(s) in what concerns need to be raised, what information needs to be shared, what interpretations need to be offered, what voices need to be heard?

⬥ What are some of the concrete steps you could take to introduce these or other transformational practices of preaching in your congregation?

⬥ Are there other transformational practices of preaching you could imagine introducing in your congregation? What would they be? How would you begin?

Resources

Budde, Mariann Edgar. *Gathering Up the Fragments: Preaching as Spiritual Practice*. Lima, Ohio: CSS Publishing Company, 2009.
  An exploration of the benefits of thinking of preaching as a spiritual discipline.

Buechner, Frederick. *Telling the Truth: The Gospel as Tragedy, Comedy, and Fairy Tale*. New York: HarperCollins Publishers, 1977.
  A classic text that explores poetically the various moods of preaching.

Campbell, Charles. *The Word Before the Powers: An Ethic of Preaching*. Louisville, Ky.: Westminster John Knox Press, 2002.
  Argues that preaching is an act of resistance to the powers and principalities embedded in our social systems.

Childers, Jana. *Performing the Word: Preaching as Theatre*.
Nashville: Abingdon Press, 1998.
  One of the first books to explore how performance practices are useful for preachers.

Childers, Jana, and Clayton Schmit, eds. *Performance in Preaching: Bringing the Sermon to Life.* Grand Rapids: Baker Publishing Group, 2008.
  An anthology of essays exploring various dimensions of sermon performance.

Davis, Ellen F. *Imagination Shaped: Old Testament Preaching in the Anglican Tradition.* Valley Forge, Penn.: Trinity Press International, 1995.
  Investigates preaching on the Old Testament by Anglican preachers, and in the last chapter describes "holy preaching" as arising from disciplined engagement with Scripture.

————. "No Explanations in the Church." In *Touching the Altar: The Old Testament for Christian Worship,* edited by Carol M. Bechtel. Grand Rapids: William B. Eerdmans Publishing Company, 2008.
  Argues for preachers to concern themselves with public issues, as the Old Testament prophets did.

————. *Wondrous Depth: Preaching the Old Testament.* Louisville, Ky.: Westminster John Knox Press, 2005.
  Demonstrates how preachers can delve more deeply into the riches of Scripture, particularly those of the Old Testament.

Florence, Anna Carter. *Preaching as Testimony.* Louisville, Ky.: Westminster John Knox Press, 2007.
  Explores testimony as an appropriate metaphor for preaching in the postmodern era.

Hauerwas, Stanley. *Performing the Faith: Bonhoeffer and the Practice of Nonviolence.* Grand Rapids: Brazos Press, 2004.
  Argues for Christian life as an ethical performance of the faith.

Johnstone, Keith. *Impro: Improvisation and the Theatre.* London: Methuen, 1981.
  A vital text for understanding the theory and practice of improvisation; contains many exercises.

Linklater, Kristin. *Freeing the Natural Voice*. Revised and expanded edition. Hollywood, Calif.: Drama Publishers, 2006.
Lays out her approach to vocal training, which aims to free and strengthen the voice through forging deeper connections between thought, feeling, breath, and body.

Roth, Nancy. *An Invitation to Christian Yoga*. Cambridge, Mass.: Cowley Publications, 2001.
Articulates a Christian approach to yoga, and offers specific yoga exercises.

Spellers, Stephanie. *Radical Welcome: Embracing God, the Other, and the Spirit of Transformation*. New York: Church Publishing, Inc., 2006.
Presents the practices of The Crossing and other emerging churches, as well as the theological principles underlying them.

Taylor, Barbara Brown. *The Preaching Life*. Cambridge, Mass.: Cowley Publications, 1993.
Conveys the joy and challenge of preaching as a spiritual practice and way of life.

Wells, Samuel. *Improvisation: The Drama of Christian Ethics*. Grand Rapids: Brazos Press, 2004.
A theological justification for improvisation as a framework for Christian ethical existence.

Notes
and Sources

NOTES TO CHAPTER ONE
1. Barbara Brown Taylor, *The Preaching Life* (Cambridge, Mass.: Cowley Publications, 1993), 76.
2. Frederick Buechner, *Telling the Truth: The Gospel as Tragedy, Comedy, and Fairy Tale* (New York: HarperCollins Publishers, 1977), 23.
3. Interview with Susan Burns, September 14, 2009.
4. David Steindl-Rast, *Music of Silence* (Berkeley, Calif.: Ulysses Press, 1998), 12.
5. Interview with Jim Bradley, August 26, 2009.
6. Interview with Ellen Davis, July 23, 2009.
7. Interview with Martin Smith, July 14, 2009.
8. See Fred Craddock, *As One Without Authority,* revised edition (St. Louis: Chalice Press, 2001); Paul Scott Wilson, *The Practice of Preaching,* revised edition (Nashville: Abingdon Press, 1995); and Richard Lischer, *A Theology of Preaching: The Dynamics of the Gospel* (Durham, N.C.: Labyrinth Press, 1992), among others.

NOTES TO CHAPTER TWO
1. Bruce Morrill, ed., *Bodies of Worship: Explorations in Theory and Practice* (Collegeville, Minn.: Liturgical Press, 1999), 1, 3.
2. Rowan Williams, *Tokens of Trust* (Louisville, Ky.: Westminster John Knox Press, 2007), 74.

3. Williams, *Tokens of Trust,* 74.

4. Williams, *Tokens of Trust,* 74.

5. Richard Ward, *Speaking from the Heart: Preaching with Passion* (Nashville: Abingdon Press, 1992), 77.

6. Marvin Carlson, *Performance: A Critical Introduction,* second edition (New York: Routledge, 2004), 5.

7. Nicholas Lash, *Theology on the Way to Emmaus* (London: SCM Press, 1986), 42.

8. Stanley Hauerwas, *Performing the Faith: Bonhoeffer and the Practice of Nonviolence* (Grand Rapids: Brazos Press, 2004), 76.

9. Charles Campbell, *The Word Before the Powers: An Ethic of Preaching* (Louisville, Ky.: Westminster John Knox Press, 2002), 79.

NOTES TO CHAPTER THREE

1. Mariann Edgar Budde, *Gathering Up the Fragments: Preaching as Spiritual Practice* (Lima, Ohio: CSS Publishing Company, 2009), 11.

2. Parker J. Palmer, *A Hidden Wholeness: The Journey Toward an Undivided Life* (San Francisco: Jossey-Bass, 2004), 77.

3. See especially Edwin H. Friedman, *Generation to Generation: Family Process in Church and Synagogue* (New York: Guilford Press, 1985), and Edwin H. Friedman, *A Failure of Nerve: Leadership in the Age of the Quick Fix* (New York: Church Publishing, 1999).

4. Budde, *Gathering Up the Fragments,* 15.

5. Ellen F. Davis, *Imagination Shaped: Old Testament Preaching in the Anglican Tradition* (Valley Forge, Penn.: Trinity Press International, 1995), 248–249. Davis draws this insight from Garrett Green, *Imagining God: Theology and the Religious Imagination* (San Francisco: Harper and Row, 1989), 109–110.

6. Ellen F. Davis, "No Explanations in the Church," in *Touching the Altar: The Old Testament for Christian Worship,* ed. Carol M. Bechtel (Grand Rapids: William B. Eerdmans Publishing Company, 2008), 97.

7. Davis, "No Explanations in the Church," 96.

8. Davis, *Imagination Shaped,* 244.

9. Ellen F. Davis, *Wondrous Depth: Preaching the Old Testament* (Louisville, Ky.: Westminster John Knox Press, 2005), 5.

10. Davis, "No Explanations in the Church," 100.

11. L. William Countryman, *Living on the Border of the Holy: Renewing the Priesthood of All* (Harrisburg, Penn.: Morehouse Publishing, 1999), xi.

NOTES TO CHAPTER FOUR

1. Kristin Linklater's approach to voice training is outlined in her *Freeing the Natural Voice,* revised and expanded edition (Hollywood, Calif.: Drama Publishers, 2006) and *Freeing Shakespeare's Voice* (New York: Theatre Communications Group, 1992).

2. Jana Childers, *Performing the Word: Preaching as Theatre* (Nashville: Abingdon Press, 1998), 49.

3. Barbara Brown Taylor, "Stand and Deliver," in *The Christian Century* (May 4, 2004).

4. Hans Georg Gadamer, *Truth and Method,* second revised edition, translation revised by Joel Weinsheimer and Donald G. Marshall (New York: Continuum Publishing Company, 1996), 361.

5. Samuel Wells, *Improvisation: The Drama of Christian Ethics* (Grand Rapids: Brazos Press, 2004).

6. Wells, *Improvisation,* 104–105.

7. Keith Johnstone, *Impro: Improvisation and the Theatre* (London: Methuen, 1981), 87–88.

8. Wells, *Improvisation,* 68.

9. I am grateful to my co-teacher, A. Katherine Grieb, professor of New Testament at Virginia Theological Seminary, for these premises for improvising on John's Gospel.

10. Wells, *Improvisation,* 80.

---

sources for quotations

Karl Barth, "The Need and Promise of Christian Preaching," in *The Word of God and the Word of Man* (New York: Harper and Row, 1928), 126.

Ellen F. Davis, *Wondrous Depth: Preaching the Old Testament* (Louisville, Ky.: Westminster John Knox Press, 2005), 2, 11.

Annie Dillard, *Teaching a Stone to Talk: Expeditions and Encounters* (New York: Harper and Row, Publishers, 1982), 40.

Anna Carter Florence, *Preaching as Testimony* (Louisville, Ky.: Westminster John Knox Press, 2007), 113.

Nora Gallagher, *Reflections,* a journal published bi-annually by Yale Divinity School, vol. 96, no. 2 (Fall 2009): 58–59.

Gwyneth Lewis, *Sunbathing in the Rain: A Cheerful Book about Depression* (London: Jessica Kingsley Publishers, 2007), 233.

Ian Pitt-Watson, *Preaching: A Kind of Folly* (Louisville, Ky.: Westminster John Knox Press, 1978).

Nancy Roth, *The Breath of God* (New York: Seabury Books, 2006), 2.

Barbara Brown Taylor, *The Preaching Life* (Cambridge, Mass.: Cowley Publications, 1993), 80.